FROM

ASHES

TO

beauty

GOD'S WAY

Kelli,

Thank you so much for your support.
I'm very grateful we reconnected!
God bless always,

Tiffany W Castleberry

FROM
ASHES
TO
beauty
GOD'S WAY

Finding God's Strength in
the Depths of Pain and Loss

Tiffany Castleberry
with J. L. GILLHAM

TATE PUBLISHING
AND ENTERPRISES, LLC

Published by Tate Publishing & Enterprises, LLC
127 E. Trade Center Terrace | Mustang, Oklahoma 73064 USA
1.888.361.9473 | www.tatepublishing.com

Tate Publishing is committed to excellence in the publishing industry. The company reflects the philosophy established by the founders, based on Psalm 68:11,
"The Lord gave the word and great was the company of those who published it."

Book design copyright © 2012 by Tate Publishing, LLC. All rights reserved.
Cover design by Kristen Verser
Interior design by Chelsea Womble

Published in the United States of America

ISBN: 978-1-62024-850-8
1. Biography & Autobiography / Personal Memoirs
2. Religion / Christian Life / Personal Growth
12.05.30

dedication

To God, my Savior, Rock, Comforter, Protector, and Prince of Peace.

Thank you for never leaving me or forsaking me!

When everyone else walks away, you are there to carry me through. I am eternally grateful.

To Daddy—my world, who was a perfect example of God's unconditional love.

In loving memory of Mom.

We had many differences, but I know you did the best you could. Thank you for the positive things you did in my life. I love you!

Also, to the one I thought was the love of my life for breaking down my walls and showing me how it truly feels to love someone unconditionally for better or worse. I wish you blessings and happiness.

acknowledgments

Every time I think of you, I give thanks to my
God. Whenever I pray, I make my requests for
all of you with joy.

Philippians 1:3-4 (NLT)

I want to take time to thank those who were there for me
most over the last couple of years. First and foremost, I
am alive only because of my faith in God. He has been
with me every step of the way, and I am eternally grateful
for his forgiveness and unconditional love.

The moment my world ended, Stefanie Hines and
Susan Johnson (my godmother) were there and haven't
left my side since.

Aunt Peggy and Aunt Sandi, I will never be able to
thank you enough for spending that horrible week with
me and not leaving. I know my daddy is so proud and
thankful.

Gini and Trey (Tigger and Pooh), thank you for
dropping everything to be with me in my darkest hour.
I love both of you and thank you from the bottom of
my heart for what you did for me then and continue to
do for me today.

I am blessed to have these people in my life as well.
They played special roles in helping me the last couple of years: Jodi Heidmous, Kelly Rodriguez, Cyrena

Stewart, Taylor Johnson (Bubba), Michelle Woodall, Charley Vaughan, Stephanie Stewart, Jason and Chrysta Sapp, James and Beth Ishmael, Kevin Passons, Jason Riley, Aunt Debbie, Cousin Karen, Cousin Kristy, Jules McGregor, J.J. Riley, Brandi Kelly, Tiffany TJ Jones, Sandy Magana, Beth Young, Melissa Galloway, Jeanette Miller, Casey Cates, Gena Weatheread, Connie "Bug" Waddell, Valeria Dawson, my EBF, Donald and our Ghost Dreams, JC, Michael Collom, Sean Burridge, Rob Scoggins, and all of my friends and prayer partners at Element Church.

Thank you to everyone who played a part in my life—good, bad, or ugly. I would not be the person I am today without you. God has a purpose for everyone, and even if you don't believe in him, he uses you.

Thank you to the countless number of people who kept me in prayer. A thousand thanks to the people who kept me laughing when I didn't know I could laugh anymore. I know there is a great possibility that I have forgotten some people. It is not because you did not help. It is simply because my memory stinks! I love you all and thank you for being there for me in your own special ways. I pray God blesses each of you and keeps you safe daily.

table of contents

Prologue 11

Not a Dream 15

Figures Hiding in the Dark 17

A Different Kind of Doll 21

So Many Changes 33

Fighting with Dad 39

The Fire of Jealousy 51

Crossing over the Threshold 59

I Blamed Myself for Everything 73

Hawaiian Coconut Coffee and Falling in Love 91

God, Don't Let Me Screw This Up 107

It's Not That Serious 121

We Need to Talk 127

Facing my Two Greatest Fears at Once 137

God Would Never Leave Me in My Darkest Hour 151

You're Not alone 169

7:03 a.m. 183

Not What I've Done but What I've Overcome 193

Right Back Where I Shouldn't Be 207

Carried by the Lord 217

Epilogue 229

prologue

I am alive. That fact astonishes me. Part of the reason is because I spent most of my existence dwelling in dangerous situations. I have endured in spite of physical and sexual abuse. In addition to these scars, like the biblical character Job, I suffered great tragedy. I've dealt with multiple medical issues and lost those who were most dear to me.

Within three days during February of 2010, my world came crashing down. My husband suddenly asked for a divorce. Before I felt like I had time to breathe, without warning my daddy died of a heart attack. I have been through a lot in my life, but facing my two greatest fears at the same time nearly ended me.

This was my darkest season. I begged God thousands of times to take me home to heaven. I didn't want to live or experience all the pain anymore. The next two years also brought with it more sexual abuse as well as my mother being diagnosed with lung cancer.

It is only by God's grace that I am living today. At times I know Christ completely carried me. My prayer is that my story would shed light on God's faithfulness and jealous love for his creation. Maybe you are going through a terrible tragedy and aren't sure if you will live to tell the tale. Maybe suicide is being considered. I've been there, and I am living proof you can survive.

My story is one filled with pain from the losses and trauma I experienced, especially during the past couple of years. In spite of the devastation, I can see the good that came out of them. The new me knows more about myself and has experienced God's faithfulness firsthand.

I am a very stubborn, determined, passionate, and strong lady. These traits helped me endure the pressures God allowed in my life. Through the pressure and heat of the trials I experienced, I am being formed. Although I feel that I am still in the rough, I'm on my way to becoming an unparalleled diamond.

If you are suffering, there is hope! No matter how horrific or painful the situation is, God is faithful. You can make it through to the other side. Don't believe me? Here is how my heavenly Father did it for me.

Mom, Dad and me Jan 1979

Mom and Dad

not a dream

Weeping may last through the night, but joy comes with the morning.

Psalm 30:5b (NLT)

That terrifying night began in the typical fashion. I had no premonition what was to come, no indication that my window that was closed and locked wouldn't be enough to keep out something sinister.

"Good night, sweetheart," my father said. Then he kissed my cheek.

"Night, Daddy." I looked up at him and grinned. He was my idol. With a sigh, I rolled over onto my left side so that I was facing my wall, clutching my king-sized pillow. I sucked my thumb and smelled the corner of the pillow while I slept. I heard a click then the door close. While my father left for his night shift at the railroad, the lights fled. It was almost like they didn't want to witness what was to come. My heavy eyelids shut, ushering me into my dreams that were typical for a second grader like myself.

Sometime during my second dream, I suddenly felt like I was under water. No one could hear me scream as I thrashed around in terror. There was no air to suck into my lungs.

"Quiet, or I'll kill you."

figures hiding in the dark

The thief's purpose is to steal and kill and destroy. My purpose is to give them a rich and satisfying life.

John 10:10 (NLT)

The gravelly voice pulled me from my imagined drowning into a living nightmare. His hand covered my nose and mouth to keep me from screaming. Shock and horror washed over me, leaving me incapable of uttering even a syllable.

I believed the monster that was crouched over my body. I didn't know if my shiver came from my nakedness or panic. The wet grass underneath me felt like seaweed. I twisted uncomfortably on the lawn from his rough touching.

Even though I couldn't speak, I heard a dog bark nearby. It sounded like Penny, the cocker spaniel. She was blind, with medium-length blond hair. The escalating noises the creature made lasted a little longer. There was a rattling sound. I didn't know if it was Charley, my best friend and the dog's owner, banging on the wall to get Penny to hush, but I was grateful for it.

The monster who'd abducted me suddenly fled. I went to the back door of my house to try and get in, but it was locked. I didn't know how he got me out, so I wasn't sure about a way to get back in.

Fear of getting in trouble for waking my mother kept me from knocking. I turned around and stumbled out the back gate and then across the alley to my best friend's house. My light tap on the front door didn't wake Charley. I worried about getting my buddy in trouble if anyone else arose from my gentle banging.

No one answered. I hurried through my back then front yard and across the street to my parents' friend's house. It was filled with males. My cheeks flushed in embarrassment from my Eve-like appearance when they opened the door.

After I was clothed, the police were called. I was chaperoned back home. It was sunrise before the men with badges finally stopped pestering me with questions. By that time, my daddy was holding me fiercely as I sat curled up in his lap.

The trauma wasn't over yet. The midday natural rays from outside were blocked by a weighty curtain in my hospital room. The doctors inspected me all over. I felt like the man in the game Operation. I didn't jolt with an electric shock if they weren't gentle enough, but occasionally a gasp or sigh escaped my lips.

In addition to dealing with the physical, my mind imagined figures hiding in every shadow. Fear coursed through my veins like blood. *Would the monster come for me again?* Then there was the apprehension of verbalizing my thoughts. I didn't want my parents to have to suffer along with me at all.

All I wanted was to let my eyelids close, taking me into a restful oblivion. When I was finally allowed to sleep, I passed out in my parents' bedroom. It was where I spent many nights during the next two years.

Shortly after the event, I decided to let my mother know what I was thinking. I sat on the closed toilet seat while she got ready in front of me.

"Mom, I remembered something about that night."

She looked at me and replied, "Oh yeah?"

"Yes. The guy that took me from my room had a smell on his hands that reminded me of daddy."

Immediately she turned. With wide eyes and a red face, she told me, "Never say that again. Do you know what that would do to your father if he knew you thought he did that?" She quickly scolded me and took what I said out of context.

"I never said I thought that. I don't think he would do that to me," I jumped in.

Mom kept on, "Don't ever speak about that again!"

We already had a bad relationship, but at that moment, I stopped trusting my mom. There would be a multitude of things that would ruin our relationship, but this I would never forget.

a different kind of doll

God is my strong fortress, and he makes my way perfect.

2 Samuel 22:33 (NLT)

As traumatic as that event was, I'd been sexually assaulted on two separate occasions before that one. The first was by a male babysitter when I was four years old. The second was by numerous classmates in the first grade.

After the abduction happened, I started acting out in school. I talked about not being a virgin, although technically I still was. At eight years old, I thought the only thing I was good for was my body. When I looked in the mirror, I didn't see a pale-faced, freckled little girl who resembled Pippi Longstockings. I saw a female to be used. I wondered, *Would anyone ever love me for anything else? Why did this abuse happen to me?*

Even though I had questions that fluttered around in my juvenile mind, nothing caused me to blame God. Dad occasionally talked about God and faith. I believed in God and was taught not to be mad at him when bad things happened.

Our family didn't go to church, but I had such a great earthly daddy in my life who always loved and comforted me. That made it easy for me to see my heavenly Father in the same light. I didn't find fault in my dad. I figured I was somehow to blame. Maybe predators really could smell fear and I emitted more than the average person, attracting the monsters in the process.

2yrs old in Dallas with Dad and Mom

After the abduction, I was sent to a rape counselor. It was horrible and just as traumatic as being molested. She forced me to *play* with dolls that had all the parts of a real body. I had to show and tell what was done to me. Speaking those words mutilated my communication process. It etched dirty and ghastly memories into my soul.

If I slept alone in my bedroom, I was given a big reward. Going a whole week afforded me a trip to the movies or a new toy I wanted. As an adult looking back, I loathe this system. It taught me to do what others asked of me, even if

I was afraid or it meant I was lying. This belief would prove hazardous as I grew into a young adult.

Modeling in Texas

My views that I was only good for my body were reinforced when I started modeling and acting. I even began attending WCCW wrestling shows with my mom. We both had fun at these events. The best times I had with my mom were without a doubt the wrestling years. The majority of the time I was running around with friends like we owned the place. My main partners in crime were Desere`, Heather, Mandy, Michael, and William.

Kerry, Chris, Me, & Desere`

We started attending them because my mom got a job with Chris Adams. I loved listening to his British accent. He was tall and had an athletic build. My mother's five-two height and petite frame looked even smaller than usual with Chris Adams or any of the muscular wrestlers around. One of her simpler tasks was to take Polaroid pictures of the wrestlers with fans during intermission.

"Say Iron Claw," she said to a pimple-faced boy standing with Kerry Von Erich.

I giggled at her use of a wrestling term replacing the standard word *cheese* usually used. Mom liked to switch up which types of moves she told the kids to say.

I studied her while she clicked the button. The left side of my lips rose slightly as I took in her joy. It was one of the few times of connecting we had together. My mom took pride in the work she did for Chris, from setting up shows to snapping those Polaroid pictures. She always tried to do her best.

I remembered another night when I witnessed a guy flirt with my mom. She tried to politely decline his advances, and then he put his hands on her.

"*****," he called her.

My eyes grew wide right before my ten-year-old tiny frame lunged at the grown man. I got my hands on him before two of the Sportatorium bodyguards grabbed me.

"You're an *******!" I shouted. "No one calls my mom a ***** except me!" I tagged on at the end. I was dead serious when I said it. Looking back now, it is pretty hilarious to imagine hearing that from a ten-year-old.

My thoughts then shifted to my father. Even though my mother and I weren't close, that didn't bother me. I was Daddy's baby girl. My relationship with my mother was more like that of peat soil while I had a granite bond with my father.

After the abuse, I would sit right next to him and hug him. However, I never felt comfortable sitting on his lap, like I sometimes saw other kids do with their fathers. I wouldn't kiss on the mouth with my parents either. It felt dirty to me after my molestation. Occasionally when I sat next to him I'd catch her staring at me with the hint of a frown on her face. I wondered if she was jealous of the attention he lavished on me.

I figured she did her best with me. I didn't want to see her in a bad light. It was hard not to though. Sometimes I had to sit with her while she got plastered at the bar then drove us home intoxicated. I wasn't all giggles and grins then. I was constantly scared for my life and praying to God the entire way home.

Daddy was my hero while she was more like a big playmate. My mother handed the picture to the kid then hurried to take the next one. Shortly after my mother started working with the wrestlers, I began as well. I looked down at my outfit, a black jacket with matching leotards. My hand gently caressed my dark hat with the red band around the rim. I liked dressing up and looking nice.

I loved the performances and the people I was able to meet. I had a huge crush on Michael, an older boy I met at the wrestling shows. He had that all-American look with blond hair that was permed in the back, and gorgeous blue eyes. He loved wrestling as much as I did. I always beat up on him because I thought that was how you flirted. Eventually, I won him over, and he became my boyfriend. He was the first boy to break my heart.

Another person I met was a pageant queen. I was introduced to her at the Sportatorium. She ushered me into her world of glamour. Sandy took me under her wing for a while, and I loved it.

"You are stunning. I believe in you," she often told me while I trained. Sandy never would've said "you're." She was always very prim and proper, which coincided with her perfect, porcelain skin. It wasn't surprising she did well in pageants with her tall, slender figure and blond hair that cascaded down her back.

Her encouragement helped me win the Cinderella pageant. The best part was learning to walk all sorts of ways and dancing for my talent portion. I always twirled in my pink poodle skirt to 1950s music, with a huge grin the entire time onstage. One year I grinned from ear to ear the entire time while performing my talent, a dance routine to Elvis's "Jailhouse Rock."

Sandy had a brother named Donald whom I enjoyed hanging out with. He was tall with an athletic build, brown hair, and matching eyes. I loved that he always had a smile on his face and a positive attitude. When I wasn't practicing my walk or talent routine, Donald and I were wrestling on the floor. He liked to whoop my butt if it was just the two of us. When he had friends over, I would pretend to be his manager. If he was losing, I would jump in and beat up on the other guy to make sure Donald would win. Those were great times. We even had our own entrance music, "Rag Doll" by Aerosmith!

Kerry Von Erich

I spent the next couple years as Chris Adams's employee, along with Mom. I was a ringette for the road shows. My job was to take the robe of the wrestler back to the dressing room when the match began. The article of clothing easily cost $2,000. Regardless of the price, it would make a great souvenir for a sneaky fan. That's why it wasn't simply tossed onto a nearby seat.

Modeling on ring

This allowed me to make friends with a lot of the wrestlers. There were many wrestlers whom I became fond of while I was a ringette: Kerry Von Erich, Rugged Rod Price, Gorgeous Gary Young, Billy Jo Travis, and

Steve Austin before he went to the WWE. I felt like I had a slew of big brothers. They were amazing.

One I felt especially close to besides Chris Adams was Terry Garvin. His nickname was "The Beauty," probably because of his long, curly brown hair and green eyes. Terry always made me feel special when I saw him. He constantly watched out for me at the road shows as well.

Terry "The Beauty" Garvin

Although I wasn't as close to Kerry Von Erich as I was to Terry Garvin, Kerry stole my heart. It wasn't only because of how handsome he was with his muscular build and long, wavy brown hair. He just had this tender-hearted aura surrounding him. He was always kind and sincere when I was around, albeit taking pictures, at road shows, or grabbing a bite to eat after the matches. I was mesmerized by Kerry Von Erich.

Mr. T, me and Kerry

"And how are you doing today?" he often asked me with a toothy grin.

"Great," I said.

"So what's your favorite subject in school?" He always showed interest in my life. Best of all, he talked to me like a grown-up. His kind words and attention earned him a large section of my heart.

Sandy and I would talk about Kerry from time to time because she knew the family personally. I didn't have the opportunity to see him very often outside of wrestling. I admired her for having that connection to him and his family.

Chris made me feel special too. I loved his British accent. I could have listened to him talk about chemistry for hours with that accent. I became close with his daughter Jade as well. We loved running around the Sportatorium after hours.

Gentleman Chris Adams

Even though there was some fun, I saw a lot of death as a young child. I was more used to attending funerals than weddings. My maternal grandmother died of lung cancer before I reached the age of double digits. When my grandmother passed away, I didn't know how to handle it. My tear ducts must've been shut off during her funeral. I didn't show a lot of emotion.

Shortly after the service, my mother had swollen eyes and a red nose from letting her sorrow flow like the rapids. I stared at Mom. Her eyes narrowed into slits. She pointed her finger at me then spoke.

"You're a cold hearted *****!"

so many changes

The LORD himself goes before you and will be
with you; he will never leave you nor forsake
you. Do not be afraid; do not be discouraged.

Deuteronomy 31:8 (NIV)

Right after her comment, my lower lip slightly jutted
out, but I kept my mouth clamped shut like a vault.
Her remark surprised me. I knew that she was grieving, but that still stung. Instead of a hug and questions
about my feelings during the loss, I got a knife to the
heart.

I didn't sob like a starving newborn like her. So I
wondered, *Is there something wrong with me? Shouldn't
I cry as much as my mother if I loved Grandma like everyone else?*

I took a deep breath then let it out. As I exhaled,
I let go of the painful memory. The ache in my heart
didn't leave, though. With so many people around me
who passed away, I started having panic attacks about
my dad. He was my savior, my warrior. *What if he was
next? Who would be there to protect and love me?*

Early one morning, while the shadows had free
reign, I woke up from a nightmare. "Dad," I mumbled,

lip quivering. I hopped off my bed and raced to my parents' room.

I reflexively closed my eyes after I whipped on the light switch. Remembering my fear, I opened them suddenly.

"What the…" my mother began.

I exhaled the breath I didn't realize I'd been holding.

"Daddy," I said. "You're okay." By this time, he was sitting up with his back against the headrest. He then repeated his usual routine. My father slowly lumbered out of bed and walked toward me. With his arm wrapped around my back and shoulders, we went back to my room.

He kneeled on the floor while I climbed into bed. After the covers were up to my shoulders, he held my face in his hands.

"Sweetie, I'm okay. Please don't worry about me."

"Okay, Daddy." I gave him my standard response, knowing that I would jump out of bed as soon as the next nightmare involving his death happened. Nothing would stop the bad dreams. Each of them were different. He never died the same way, and it made me so paranoid.

One time in 1989 while my father was at work, there was an incident. It didn't kill him, thankfully, but it did cause permanent damage. Daddy went to work on the railroad on a night like every other. A few hours after being there, something terrible happened. Years earlier they would use torpedo bombs on the tracks when two trains were on the same track. They outlawed the use of the torpedo bomb for various reasons. This night some kids apparently got a hold of a two torpedoes and placed them on the train tracks.

My dad wasn't that far away from them. The first one went off, and he grabbed his left ear and turned around as the second one went off. Daddy was bleeding from both of his ears and was immediately taken to the closest ER. He lost 60 percent of his hearing out of both ears and was medically retired from the railroad.

In 1990, my parents decided to relocate. Between seventh and eighth grade, we moved to Gun Barrel City, Texas. By this point, my relationship with my mom hadn't improved any. In fact, it got worse every year.

"Tiffany, we need to go," she said as she rapidly waved her hand back and forth. It was my last day of school with all my friends in Cedar Hill.

"But, wait. I wanted to say good-bye." My eyebrows formed a loose *V*. I looked up at her with large eyes.

"Now," was her quick reply.

"I…I haven't had a chance say good-bye to everyone."

"You'll make new friends."

I obediently towed behind her with my head hung low. *What did I do to deserve this?* I climbed into the car then stared at the school for the last time until it was only a memory.

I pictured Charley, my best friend, standing on the curb looking for me. There'd be no chance to thank him for being such a loyal friend and always being there for me. *God, please comfort Charley since I can't tell him I love him*, I prayed.

One of the places I learned the importance of prayer was in church. Sometimes I went with another friend,

Erin, and her family. I loved feeling part of a family while we sang songs to God. My heart glowed with warmth when I was done. I would need the comfort to get me through the next phase of life.

My eighth grade class was one-fourth the size I was used to. I was bullied and had a hard time making new pals. Joelene, one of my friends from my previous school, even wrote me to say her parents would let me live with them if I wanted to return. But my hopes were crushed when my own mom and dad said no.

It wasn't long after my eighth grade year started that I realized just how much I wanted to go back to Cedar Hill. I never had a hard time making friends with males, but females were a different story completely. The majority of the females thought I was only friends with their boyfriends to steal them. Therefore, it wasn't long until I had girls telling me they wanted to kick my butt.

One particular day after lunch I went out to the courtyard. Shortly after I walked outside, three girls came up to me and got in my face, yelling at me, "Go back to where you came from!" They threatened to kick my butt if I didn't watch what I was doing. I wanted to be there about as much as they wanted me there. I hated the new small town I was in and tried to go back and visit my friends in Cedar Hill as often as possible.

The few bright spots on the otherwise overcast days in my life were spent boating and swimming at the nearby lake. I made a few friends who graduated to high school with me. My days moving from a freshman to a senior passed by, like flipping through pages of a yearbook.

During my freshman year, I dated John. He wasn't even a fraction of the man my father was. Unfortunately that didn't keep me from my boyfriend. The hunky, Mexican football player with brown eyes was in the popular crowd. I accompanied him to a Halloween party one Saturday night.

He was huddled with a group of guys while I talked with other people on the sidewalk. I admired all the ghouls and ghosts that drifted by; then I glanced down at my simple jeans. I'd outgrown dressing up in a costume years before.

"Hey, baby. Gimme a kiss," John said.

"No, thanks," I replied, thinking about how he uncharacteristically had a cigarette. Usually he only dipped Skoal, but this evening he smoked with his friends.

"I said give me a kiss!"

"Yuck. Not after what's been in your mouth." I began walking away. When I was halfway down the driveway, the back of my head felt like it'd exploded. My body flew forward, ramming me into the parked black Mustang.

fighting with dad

Jesus answered him, I assure you, most solemnly I tell you, that unless a person is born again (anew, from above), he cannot ever see (know, be acquainted with, and experience) the kingdom of God.

John 3:3 (AMP)

It wasn't a bomb that had exploded, causing my flight. As I pulled myself up, three of John's friends raced toward me. They all had the same wide eyes. Except their fright didn't come from any nearby haunted houses.

"Tiffany, please don't tell anyone what happened," said the first one to reach me. My date was leaning against the vehicle a few feet away, his hands clenched and eyes narrowed.

"You'll be okay," the second one added. "John has a temper, but he's a good guy. Really." I knew they were only concerned about him playing in the next big game, not the growing bump on the back of my head.

Little did his groupies know they had nothing to worry about. Because of my past, I never would have turned him in. Whenever bad things happened to me, I felt like I deserved it. I didn't blame the perpetrator. Instead I sentenced myself to feelings of worthlessness.

I stayed with the football player even though I felt far from a rescued damsel.

"You're worthless," he said, spitting the words at me Thanksgiving Day. The wind whipped my hair around my face as we walked to his front door.

I wrapped my arms around myself to keep off the chill. My light sweatshirt wasn't enough. Instead of grabbing my jacket out of my hall closet, I'd raced to John's car. *What if he leaves if I make him wait more than a couple seconds?* I thought. Now that we'd arrived I couldn't do anything about my cold state.

"You're lucky to be going out with me. You're a whore, and no one else would ever want you." He ran his fingers through his hair and avoided eye contact. I waited with him, rubbing my arms rapidly.

"John, please," I begged. I wanted him to care for me not berate me. I stared into his chocolate eyes, wishing my love would make them melt like my heart did for him.

Instead of apologizing, he glared at me. "You're *ugly* and don't deserve *me*." He broke eye contact and glanced through the bay window into his house.

When we went inside, we ate Thanksgiving dinner with his parents. They were always so welcoming every time I visited. We pretended everything was perfect. Our conversation picked up right where it left off in his room after we'd eaten.

"You're a jerk!" I yelled at him. I was fed up with his name-calling.

"Watch the way you speak to me." He lifted his hand to strike me.

"Keep it down, you two!" his mother shouted from the other side of his door after she lightly rapped on it three times. I assumed she thought we were playing around. If we were, I wouldn't have left his house that night with a new bruise. He knew exactly how to hit me and where so there wouldn't be any visible marks to my friends and family.

During another conversation, John tried to talk me into getting on birth control so I would have sex with him. This led to my first serious fight with my dad. I had quietly discussed getting on birth control with my mom. I thought since she got pregnant at seventeen she would be easy to convince.

My dad ended up walking into the kitchen while we were talking about it. Mom told him what I was asking, and he blew a gasket. He was yelling, "My daughter will *not* get on birth control in high school!" My dad never yelled at me because he knew all he had to do was raise his voice and I would start crying. This was different. At first I started to yell back.

"It's not fair. I'm just trying to be safe. I don't want to end up like Mom and pregnant at seventeen!"

Dad's face turned red like a tomato, and he said, "No!" and that was it. I stopped arguing and went to my room and cried. I couldn't believe I let a stupid boy cause me to get in a fight with my dad. It broke my heart to fight with my father.

Shortly after that, John broke up with me. If he hadn't, I don't know when I would have gotten away. I thought I deserved his abuse. *Why else would someone do that to me?*

In addition to dealing with my thoughts of self-hatred, I had my mother's cruel comments to fend off. Our arguing got a little more heated a few weeks after John and I broke up. When my father got home one evening, I skipped over to him.

"Dad, look," I beamed as I handed him my report card full of A's. The one next to the line that read Spanish class made me the proudest. I enjoyed studying another language and worked hard on my enunciation.

"You're just trying to make me look bad," my mother chimed in as she walked toward us.

"What?" I asked incredulously. I knew my own mother wasn't going to congratulate me for my hard work paying off. I blocked her from snatching it out of my father's hand.

"That's great, honey. I'm really proud of you." He smiled as he read each line.

"So you think you're better than me because of a piece of paper?"

"Whatever." I stomped off.

I usually spent most of my time with friends. I didn't like to bring them home much, though. Mom tried to hang out with us like she was just a teenager. One evening we got into a big fight. I walked into the living room and faced both my parents sitting on the couch.

"Mom, I'm tired of you acting like you are one of us. You think it's cool to hang out with my friends when you're trashed, and it's not okay." I stood in front of my mother with my hands on my hips.

"Martha, she's right. You need to give her space and let her have time with her friends." I was glad to have my father's support.

"You always take her side!" she said; then she straightened her back. Maybe it was done so I was reminded my mom was superior to me.

I knew what was coming. She wanted to start wrestling. I quickly dropped her to the ground. She got in a few good hits, but that wouldn't last long. I was quick tempered and would get enraged after a couple of hits. A ring wasn't needed, and my dad refused to be our referee.

"I think this is a bad idea," he stated as usual.

Since my mother ignored his attempt at stopping us, I kept up defending myself. We took our bouts seriously. She had me pinned on the ground with her knees on top of my shoulders. I swung my legs up and grabbed her head. Then I pulled her back to the ground and put her in a scissor lock, squeezing her abdomen. An onlooker might've thought these moves were playful, but we were both all business.

After ten minutes, I won that round. I sat in the corner to catch my breath. I never allowed myself that privilege during our fights. I was too stubborn to stop to fully fill my lungs. That would've given her time to do the same thing.

"Don, why didn't you jump in to help me?" she asked, touching the right side of her face that was red from one of my smacks.

"I'm not tangling on the floor with my daughter. I never want to see one bruise on her face."

Just because they were married didn't mean my dad was exempt from the harsh words Mom spewed out like vomit. "You always take her side," she continued. She gave him a hateful look and stormed off like a spoiled three-year-old who didn't get her way.

I hated to see him suffer. "Leave him out of this," I said. Recently I'd begun provoking her whenever she began picking on my father. I would've wrestled her until she was too exhausted to speak if that was what it would have taken to protect my father from her.

If Daddy was ever in danger from Mom or anyone else, I would've used my body or my words to protect him. I doubted it would come to it, but I wouldn't have hesitated to lay down my life for my hero. *What was my existence worth compared to his anyway?*

Even though my dad was still around, I had to suffer the loss of someone I cared about deeply. In 1993, my muscled friend Kerry Von Erich committed suicide. When I found out, I ran to my bedroom and locked the door behind me. I spent the next two days crying in my self-imposed prison.

By this time I usually didn't tear up when people expected me to. I did my best to cut off my emotions after the abuses I'd already suffered. I didn't want to feel the pain.

Sometimes I looked to God to help me with what I felt. One safe haven from the tragedies I was dealing with and my frustrations with my mother was with my high-school age church youth group. We went to Lake

Lavon Church Camp the summer between my freshman and sophomore year. I had a blast. Shortly after, I got serious about my relationship with Jesus. That was when I started paying attention to God. I wanted to follow him, even if it meant I was different. That didn't matter because I began to feel God close to me.

In July of 1994, I went to lunch at a local Mexican restaurant after church with my friend Courtney and her family. There wasn't anything special about this particular day until a guy walked in the door and caught my eye. We were sitting there talking when the hostess started walking another larger church group by our table. I glanced up and was captivated by the young man walking in front of me. He was tall (to me) with light-brown hair and had an astounding smile and this aura of confidence that fascinated me. It was as if everything turned to slow motion as I watched him walk all the way to the table they were seated at, and I'm pretty sure my mouth was open.

I had seen good-looking guys before, but none whom I felt drawn to. I noticed he was sitting with Brad, someone I went to school with. So Monday at school I looked for Brad. I asked, "Who was the guy with the light-brown hair and green eyes you were with at lunch yesterday?"

He kind of chuckled and said, "Oh, that was Paul and his family. We go to church together."

"How can I meet him?" I asked. I didn't care how forward that was. I had to meet him and learn what he was all about.

"Come to church Wednesday, and I'll introduce you."

You better believe I was there early Wednesday and trying to look my best. Brad kept his promise and introduced me to Paul. We exchanged numbers, back when there weren't cell phones in everyone's pocket, and started talking every night. Paul didn't go to my school or live in my town. He was about twenty minutes away and went to a small school in Malakoff.

"I love you," Paul told me after a week.

"What? You're a liar!" I didn't even think. I just blurted it out. Immediately I felt horrible for just squashing another person's feelings like that.

"I'm sorry. You just caught me completely off guard," I said. I couldn't understand how anyone would feel that way about me after a week. Thankfully, he forgave me, and we moved on.

I heard someone make a comment about Paul and his age but wasn't sure exactly what was said. So the next time I was on the phone with him, I asked, "How old are you?"

He got quiet and asked, "Why? What made you ask that?"

"Just tell me your age," I replied.

After about ten seconds of silence, he slowly responded, "I'm twelve."

"*What?*" I quickly yelled. I was a sixteen-year-old sophomore in high school completely smitten with a twelve-year-old seventh grader? He was always with the upper classmen from my school. Why would the juniors be hanging out with a seventh grader?

I found out quickly the guys from my school had a crush on Paul's sister. She was a couple of years older than me, and then it all made sense. I thought since he was at another school I would be safe from jokes and ridicule. It only took a few weeks for news to travel in our tiny town, and my guy friends had a field day picking on me.

Paul and I started going out July 31, 1994. On September 10, 1994, I officially gave my life to God through praying the salvation prayer. I asked him to be in control of my life. I also wanted him to save me from not only an eternity without him but also from living my life on earth without his help. God and I both knew I needed to be saved from myself.

My relationship with God and Paul was going good until October. Paul and I broke up for two months. After I found out how young Paul was and my friends started with the jokes, I played it off like it wasn't anything serious. I cheated on him with an ex-boyfriend one night. The problem with him knowing a lot of people from my school was he also heard the rumors. It didn't take long for him to hear I cheated on him.

Originally when he asked me about what I did, I lied. I do not respond well to confrontation, and as a defense mechanism I lied, hoping it would just go away. My lie just backfired on me as usual. Eventually I owned up to it, and he broke up with me. I spent the next two months begging and sweet-talking my way back into his good graces. It took work, but with a little help from the song "On Bended Knee" by Boys II Men, we got back together on January 7, 1995.

This time I swore not to take him for granted. He stole my heart, and for the first time I was in love and very happy. Paul was so sweet and caring. He was my best friend. I told him everything daily, but not about my past. I didn't really acknowledge the abuse in my history and rarely discussed it.

On February 18, we went on a retreat with our church to Pineywoods, Texas. We were in the church van driving the two hours to Pineywoods when Paul kissed me for the first time! I was a happy girl for a couple of reasons. First, I couldn't believe I had been going out off and on with someone for seven months and never touched but happy he wasn't focused on that. Second, he was very respectful about it all. He asked to kiss me before he did it. It was so sweet.

We were great and happy for the next five months. In June, his family was taking a three-week driving vacation. We were both so sad about not being able to talk or see each other for the entire time. Paul and I sat and talked for hours at his house the night before they left. He walked me out to my car, and when I looked up at him, he was crying. My heart sank, and we hugged for a few minutes.

"I love you and hate the thought of being away from you for so long," he told me.

I looked at his tear-filled eyes and said, "We will be fine. Have fun, and I will see you when you get home!"

It sucked not talking to my best friend or seeing him for three weeks, but time went by. I was so excited for the day they returned. Something changed… Paul was different when they got home from their vacation. I couldn't put my finger on it, but he was distant.

A week later, we left for Glorieta, New Mexico, south of Santa Fe, where our church camp was that summer. It was about a twelve-hour bus ride, but thankfully we had a charter bus so it was a little more comfortable than a school bus. Paul and I sat together and talked, but things were still different. He wasn't the same guy that a month earlier was crying and upset about not seeing me for three weeks.

At first, our youth group was having a great time. One night toward the end of our week, I couldn't find Paul. We had our nightly devotion time with the entire group. As much as I didn't want to be late, I wanted to know where my boyfriend was. I had a bad feeling, so I grabbed two of our mutual friends, Derek and Jeremy, to go looking for him.

I heard a lot of couples went down Pulpit Road at night to make out. Something inside of me told me to go there first.

I could see on Jeremy's face he knew something bad was about to happen. We stopped at the end of Pulpit Road, and I saw Paul and some girl walking our direction.

the fire
of jealousy

Place me like a seal over your heart, like a seal
on your arm. For love is as strong as death, its
jealousy as enduring as the grave. Love flashes
like fire, the brightest kind of flame.

Song of Solomon 8:6 (NLT)

My body instantaneously believed it was on fire. I
lost all good judgment as he turned off Pulpit Road.
Even though I saw the female, I focused on Paul and
decided to save her for later. I hastily walked up to
Paul and started screaming all kinds of words a person
should never say at church camp, or anywhere else for
that matter.

"What were you doing with her?" I asked.

"Nothing. We were just talking."

I knew he'd lied straight to my face. I was about
three inches from Paul's face when I bellowed, "Liar!"

A moment later I saw our youth pastor walking up.
At that instant, I remembered we were late for devo-
tions. I became reprehensibly aware of the words everyone around us had heard me say. In a split second, I was
mortified at my actions. Our pastor said we needed to
come with him so they could start devotion time.

We all walked into the room, and all eyes were on Paul and me. For the first time in a year, we parted like the Red Sea and took chairs on opposite sides of the room. His cousin looked at me from across the room and mouthed, "Are you okay?"

As tears filled my eyes, I shook my head no. They tried to lead us in our devotion, but no one in the room could focus. I was visibly upset and crying. Paul was sitting slouched with his arms crossed tightly against his stomach and staring at the floor. The moment we finished our closing prayer, his cousin looked at him and yelled, "What did you to do her?" and ran over to me.

Some of the people cleared out of the room while we were in a circle with our friends in the middle of the room.

Over and over, I asked Paul, "What did you do?"

He finally looked at me and said, "We just kissed." His tone was utterly nonchalant. My heart broke as I lost the strength to stand up and fell in the chair behind me.

Memories came rushing back to me about cheating on Paul over nine months earlier. Of course I tried to justify it by telling myself that we weren't serious so it wasn't as cutting. Now we were in love and had been together for nearly a year.

I cried myself to sleep that evening in absolute disbelief of the night's events. I replayed everything that happened incessantly in my head. I woke up the next morning with burning, puffy eyes from hours of crying. The first thought in my head was to find the girl.

It didn't take long, and I discovered her. I asked, "Did you know the person you were with last night was my boyfriend?"

"No," she said while she played confused.

I proceeded to give her more information. Then I asked her, "How old are you?"

"Sixteen. Why?"

My response was spiteful, "Oh, because he's thirteen!" Inside I was smiling because I knew that didn't go over well with her. "He's my boyfriend, and I would appreciate you staying away from him," I told her simply.

One problem was dealt with, but now I needed to talk to my boyfriend about what was going on. I went to his room, but he had a couple of other guy friends with him. He was lying on the bed, so I politely asked, "Paul, will you please come talk to me?"

"I'm not in the mood."

So I went ahead and asked with everyone in the room, "Why did you cheat on me?"

Jayson, our mutual friend, quickly chimed in with, "You cheated first. You deserved it."

In spite of the facts in that statement, I was stunned and hurt. Did he really believe that I deserved him to do that to us? Maybe I did deserve every bad thing that happened to me.

On our bus ride home, Paul started messing with me. I got irritated after a while and said, "If you touch me again, no matter how hard or soft, I'm gonna punch you in the face." We were about a quarter mile from the church parking lot. We got off the bus, and Paul touched my leg again. I turned around without thinking it through and punched him in the eye.

It was the first time I had ever raised my hand to another person in that way. Instantly there was a black dot on his eye. I looked at him and said, "I told you not to touch me again." However, I knew I didn't hit him because he touched my leg. I hit him because he cheated on me at church camp and I was heartbroken.

Paul and I broke up three weeks later because I was having nightmares about him cheating, and he didn't seem even a little remorseful about it. Of course I blamed myself for him cheating and us breaking up. I lost my best friend when I lost Paul.

I was sitting in my bedroom criticizing myself for losing him. Ultimately I got up off my bed and stood in front of the mirror looking at the disheveled person with tears rolling down her face. I said, "It's all your fault," to the girl in the mirror and repeatedly started punching myself in the face.

It was as if I thought I needed to be punished for losing him. Therefore, if no one else was going to do it, I should do it myself. I punched myself in the face countless times until I couldn't take the pain any more. When I was done, I had a swollen cheek and the right side of my face was black and blue.

I hid the bruises from my parents with makeup and my hair. I had no idea how I would explain it to them. If I said I did it, they would freak, but if I said someone else did it, my dad would hunt them down. As for my friends, I couldn't admit I did it to myself because they would all think I was crazy. For that reason, I told them a random guy I met at the Square did it. My friends wouldn't go hunt someone down; they would just feel bad for me.

If news got back to Paul, I thought, *Maybe he will be sympathetic and we'll get back together.* I knew what I did was wrong, and I knew my thought process was beyond questionable, but what else could I do? It was better than the other thoughts I was having about driving into a tree or telephone pole so I would end up in the hospital. I knew that was crazy and complete stupidity.

The bruises were already on my face, so I had to have some kind of story because I knew I wouldn't be able to hide them from everyone. I have no idea what Paul thought because we never got back together. I was depressed for months, but as with all of my other feelings, I stuffed them down and put a lid on them. I compared every guy and relationship to him. I knew the greatest relationships were the ones where you were best friends because it added something special.

Besides Paul, I always had guy friends I hung out with. I wasn't an athletic person in junior high or high school. I loved to play volleyball, but being five two didn't make me a star player. So I volunteered to be the boys' basketball manager in high school. I started my freshman year and continued all four years. Since I got along better with males versus females, it only made sense for me to be the boys' manager.

Mom and me before prom

As with everything in life, it had its ups and downs, but overall I loved every minute of it. My freshman year it was a dream job since the seniors I had a crush on were basketball players.

The first three years were a blast but nothing spectacular. It was my senior year that meant the most. The coach was awesome and made me feel like a member of the team. Although I knew most of the varsity players from previous years, we bonded and built friendships that would span decades to come that year.

What was most important about that job and these guys was for the first time since I moved to Gun Barrel City, I felt like I belonged. JC, Heath, James, and Jason accepted me for the goofy odd ball I was. JC, Heath, and Jason had an athletic build while James was more stocky. They all had brown eyes and all loved to pick on me. Oh man, but did they live up to something my dad once told me: "Baby girl, people wouldn't pick on you if they didn't love you!"

On away games, these hoodwinks seemed to always find a way to make me look like a perfect fool. It was always in good fun, and I knew that. When I wasn't infatuated with some jerk, these were the guys I wanted to hang out with. Over the years, they would prove to be true friends.

Heath and James joined the Marine Corps after high school, but we did well at keeping in touch from time to time. Jason went off to college, and JC was off racing cars somewhere. No matter which direction everyone went, we always found our way back home. They will always be my friends and hold a special place in my heart!

crossing over the threshold

Lean on, trust in, and be confident in the Lord
with all your heart and mind and do not rely on
your own insight or understanding.

Proverbs 3:5 (AMP)

One night when the spring flowers were barely pop-
ping their heads above ground, I got home late. I figured I'd be in trouble for breaking curfew, but there was
no one else around. I heard the garage door creaking.
I peeked through the blinds and saw both cars pulling
up. It wasn't difficult to make out the sounds of screaming that came from their direction.

It was uncommon to hear *both* of them having
a yelling match. My heart raced when I plucked my
name out of the heated conversation.

"It has nothing to do with Tiffany," came the husky voice.
I didn't know what was going on until he continued.

"I can't believe I caught you all over another man in
a bar." Images of my mother making eye contact with a
stranger flooded my vision. I shook my head in an attempt
to free myself from letting the mental show continue.

"Well, I don't want to hold your hands, so I found
someone else's to grab on to."

"That's it. We're getting a divorce," he stated.

A gasp escaped my lips. I knew they didn't always get along, but this was a surprise. As the knob turned to let them into the house, I hurried to my room before they caught me eavesdropping.

How dare she do that to him! I was so angry I wanted to take a sledgehammer to her car. I knew my father wasn't perfect, but he was a great man. He provided for us, was encouraging and supportive, and his eyes twinkled when he smiled. Why couldn't she see he was a diamond worth keeping, not discarding like a cubic zirconium?

The next day I found out the guy she made out with wasn't just a random stranger. He was a cousin of one of my good friends. That added to the humiliation and gave me more reasons to loathe her. After that night, I treated my mother like a leper. If she didn't want anything to do with my father, I wasn't going to have much of a relationship with her either.

They separated shortly after the event. By then, I only had six weeks of school left. I'd decided spring of my junior year to sign up for the delayed enlistment program. The plan was for me to go into the air force after graduation. My father was a Vietnam veteran and very patriotic. Part of my decision came from my desire for my dad to not have to support me any longer or pay for my college education. I was so grateful for the ways he did more than most parents. I owed it to him to make something of myself.

I was going to basic training in August. I stayed with my dad until I had to leave. I wanted to bask in his love until the final second.

The last week before I had to give him a hug good-bye, I constantly begged God to keep him safe. "Please, please, please protect my father from harm," I'd begin. "God, I need my daddy. I don't know how I'll get by without him." He was my north star, the foundation that kept me from cracking. I couldn't survive if he wasn't breathing somewhere on this earth.

How will I know he's all right if we don't live together anymore? I constantly worried about reaching him when I didn't live with him anymore. It was difficult living away from him. If my dad didn't answer the phone, I freaked out and had a panic attack until I got a hold of him.

My daddy was my world and my best friend. He had all the answers to everything and always knew how to console me when I was upset. He was the best earthly example of God the Father. I was blessed because he loved me unconditionally, just like God does.

I'd never respected a man the way I did my dad. He was tender and loving. Whenever I came home from playing with the neighborhood kids with a scratched-up knee, he gently patched me up. One Saturday morning I got home and told my dad a neighborhood boy wanted to beat me up.

"You go back and whoop his butt," he began as he looked at me calmly. "Or you're going to get a whooping from me when you get home!" I whooped that little boy good. There was no way I would've given my daddy a reason to spank me.

Don't get me wrong. We had our disagreements. If I needed it, he wouldn't hesitate to put me in my place.

We had an amazing father-daughter relationship. I was so proud of my daddy, and he was my hero.

For the most part, basic training was a blur. However, one thing I will never forget is my TI (technical Instructor) TSgt Driver. He was agitated with me after lunch one day. Before I could get out the door, he stopped me and stood less than six inches from my face. He looked me dead in the eyes and said, "Your face makes me nauseous!"

It took everything I had to keep my mouth shut and not start crying right there. I rushed up to our dorm and ran to the bathroom. As soon as I entered the door, I started bawling. I could not believe anyone would say that to another human being.

Basic Training graduation 1997

After I finished basic training, I was in the services career field working in lodging. I got stationed at Cannon AFB, New Mexico, in 1997.

One night I had a horribly realistic nightmare. When I woke up, I called Dad at his home in Texas. I couldn't just drive to his house and check on him. He didn't answer.

"I can't come in yet," I told my supervisor over the phone.

"Okay, Tiffany. What's wrong?" my supervisor asked with kindness in his voice.

"I can't come in until I get a hold of my dad." I wanted to hurry so I could redial my father.

"Is something wrong with him? Is he in the hospital?"

"No. I just need to make sure he's okay."

"There's nothing wrong? Why are you worried then?"

"I'm sorry. I really need to hang up so I can reach him."

Twenty minutes later I finally talked to my father. I was hysterical by this point.

"Tiffany, I'm okay. Please don't agonize over me, sweetie."

"Oh, Daddy. I was so worried." I didn't care if I got in trouble at work because they didn't understand. All that mattered was that I still had that one person my life revolved around. It was like Saturn's rings worrying their planet would disappear.

"Tiffany, you can't get upset every time you don't hear from me right away." I imagined he was rubbing the back of his neck while gently reprimanding me. This was the usual incident that involved him scolding me.

"If you pass away while I'm alive, I won't survive."

"Don't talk like that. You are a tough young lady. Besides, it's not something you need to think about."

If I got serious with a boyfriend, I made sure he knew that I would be inconsolable if anything happened to my dad. I knew whomever I was with would have a difficult job taking care of me if my worst fear came true.

In 1998, I went on my first deployment as an enlisted services person to Kuwait. I was nineteen years old and had never been away from my dad longer than six weeks. And that was basic training! My group was given twenty-four-hour notice and told we couldn't tell our family or friends.

"Dad," I could barely get another word out. Tears made the phone slippery as it rested against my right ear.

"Hey, baby girl. Is everything all right?"

It was so good to hear his voice. I pictured him sitting at the kitchen table reading a Tom Clancy book.

"I can't tell you where I'm going, but I have to leave right away." I wiped my cheeks with my shirtsleeve, unconcerned with wetting the material. "I'm going to be gone for so long."

"I'm proud of you, sweetie. You are a tough airman, and I know you can make it."

"Thanks, Daddy."

"Just know on those long days that I'm home praying for you."

I clenched my eyes shut, spilling out the pooling liquid. His encouragement was like food after a week-long fast. I knew it was hard on him since I was his baby girl and only child. He didn't let it show. He kept his tone upbeat.

"Stay safe, okay?"

"You got it." I took one deep breath and then hung up the phone after our good-byes.

Less than three days later my team landed at a bare base site. Our female captain, nicknamed Firecracker because of her red hair and brash attitude, shouted at us, "You will be erecting your own tents for a place to sleep tonight or you'll all be on the ground."

They were GP Medium Temper tents. At surge capacity, you could sleep sixteen, but thankfully we only slept twelve in each. It was 0200, and we were exhausted but didn't have a choice about getting our temporary lodging up.

The experience was as different as I could've imagined. My training helped prepare me for it mentally, though. At that moment, I was actually grateful for all of the hours we spent putting tents up at technical school.

My coworkers and I worked our butts off. We were up with the sun and didn't finish our duties until late at night. Many days were eighteen hours of straight work. The first month we didn't even get one day off. Even though I deployed with an M-16, they stayed in the armory the entire time. It didn't feel dangerous, except for early one morning.

A typical day, after we set up the base with tents and people arrived, was getting to work at 0600 to start serving breakfast. We worked twelve-hour days six days a week running the DFAC, recreation tent, movie tent, weight room, and BX. We were busy but made sure to enjoy our off time as much as we could.

During my hours off, I tried to spend time with a Navy SEAL I had met. He was the most handsome man I had ever seen. He had beautiful naturally curly blond hair and gorgeous blue eyes. I had an enormous schoolgirl crush on Ryan. He was built perfectly. There were muscles everywhere, but not over the top.

When I wasn't able to spend time with Ryan, I would hang out with the Pavelow crew who lived in the tents across from mine. They were hilarious and would invite me over to play cards. They taught me how to play Spades and Hearts. Spades was the best and it was even better when I was winning.

That is when I met Lt. Col Tommy Hull, the funniest and most down-to-earth US Air Force Academy grad I would ever meet. All the helicopter pilots were friendly and looked after me when guys would come around. They were another group of big brothers I acquired.

I had so much respect for Lieutenant Colonel Hull. I made sure to keep in touch with him from time to time. Those guys played a huge part in making that deployment the best experience.

Around 0530, the majority of the base woke up to a panicked airman on the base intercom freaking out.

"Incoming attack…" were all the words I heard. The poor kid was all over the place and couldn't seem to complete a sentence. We grabbed our chemical warfare bags and ran to the closest bunker. We were all trying to figure out what was going on, and most were in a panic state.

A few of us girls were at the end of the bunker talking among ourselves.

"I'm nineteen years old and can't die a virgin!" Adrienne looked at us with a dead-serious face. The other three of us felt that way too. We thought we might die soon, and that's what we were worried about at that moment!

We didn't want to die as virgins. We were told a missile was launched from Pakistan and was coming our way. It didn't take long to find out the night shift didn't pass on to the day shift that Pakistan was doing a practice launch. We were never in any danger. The entire experience was worth it though. After it was all over, I felt proud to call myself an airman.

In June of 1998, I went back to Cannon Air Force Base and worked in lodging as a front desk clerk. I met a lot of great people while I was deployed. Some of them were stationed at Hurlburt Field, Florida. I decided to take leave and go visit a few of them in August. I was so excited. At first, it was great seeing everyone again. I was very naïve at nineteen years old. I thought I would go visit friends and maybe do some harmless flirting with hot guys.

I stayed with "Meat" and thought it would be fun hanging out. He had different motives. One night we had been out and drinking a lot, and he started kissing me. Meat wanted to take it much farther, but I had no intention of anything sexual at all. He was about six seven and close to three hundred pounds—a big boy.

He tried to force me to have sex. I squirmed around and cried. I kept saying, "Please, no!" I stood no chance of fighting him off. I just kept praying he would stop.

He eventually stopped and passed out. I felt so uncomfortable after that. I stayed with other friends until I drove back to New Mexico.

I was notified in the fall of 1998 that I had been selected for an assignment in Belgium. I was going to SHAPE (Supreme Headquarters Allied Powers Europe). The four-star general at the time was Wesley Clark, who ran for president after he retired. On April 19, 1999, I left for my new home.

I was assigned under General Clark in his mess. I worked with two German chefs, two British waiters, two army NCOs, and a Belgian waitress. The German's were not happy to find out how little training I had when it came to cooking. I was by no means a qualified chef. Therefore, they looked at sending me to Paris or London to attend Le Cordon Bleu Culinary School.

I really enjoyed working with the different nationalities and loved traveling around Europe. I was in country less than twenty-four hours before I met an interesting person who ended up being my best friend. Nick, my sponsor, took me to the base club my first night in Belgium. I was jet lagged and disoriented, to say the least. I am known for making a horrible first impression. I'm extremely shy and quiet, which tends to translate to others as stuck up *****. Knowing this, you would think I would be less critical of others initially, but no, I'm not.

So I was sitting at the club with Nick, and I saw this girl on the dance floor. She was dancing really trashy. My first impression was, "Oh, she has to be a hoochie!"

She came and sat down at our table and then started talking to the people around me. I looked at her round face and brown eyes. I heard her name was Gini, and I tried to be cordial. The next night a group of us, including Gini, went to downtown Mons and hung out. I have a picture from that night, and you can tell we did not look comfortable together.

I laugh looking back now because only a couple of days later we were good friends and became inseparable. Gini was the first of my soon to come Winnie the Pooh family. Gini was Tigger with her constant upbeat outlook. Later I would become Piglet because I was the obvious small one of the group.

Gini and me in the barracks in Belgium

I would not only make friends while there but also enemies. After about three weeks of being at work, the chief warrant officer four in our chain of command asked for a ride to his officer quarters. I don't remember the reasoning behind it, but I gave him a ride. When we got there, he tried to kiss and hit on me. I made a complaint at work. No one believed me, and I instantly became the black sheep. My employment went downhill from there.

After about four months, I left the Mess for main base SHAPE. I worked at the fitness center for the next two years. I loved the opportunity to work with four Brits, one Dutchman, two Germans, and one Belgian woman. There is nothing like working with the international community.

I continued the pattern I'd formed when I was younger of dating guys who were abusive. In June of 1999, I began talking with James. I loved his Long Island talk and attitude he'd picked up since he grew up there. His pale-white skin allowed all of the dramatic-colored tattoos to be easily noticeable. He was part of the military police in the army. The fact that he was five years older than me and was rumored to beat his soon-to-be ex-wife didn't stop me from spending time with him.

That gossip should've been a red flag to someone like me, but I thought I could change people back then. I always wanted to be that special girl to tame the bad boy.

In August, another member of our family arrived. Trey, AKA Pooh, was welcomed into the family. With Gini and Trey now in my life, I would never be able to see friends the same way again. They were loyal and dependable like I never knew before. Don't get me wrong. We had our fights like all friends do, but I could not shake those two if wanted to.

Me n Gin in CO2

We were inseparable, and everyone knew us. We went out constantly and danced up a storm at the clubs on both bases. Then we met Connie and inducted her into the family immediately. She was full of life, gorgeous with her light-blond hair, and always wore a huge smile. She was Kanga because she had four children of her own and was motherly to everyone around her. They would prove to be my only saving graces while in Europe.

Later that month I spent time with James at a bar. "If you hit me, I'll kill you," I told him over drinks. "I'm not playing games." It was a bluff, but I thought it might keep me from getting bruises. It deterred him from striking me but not from something worse.

I asked James point-blank, "Did you hit your ex-wife? Are any of the rumors about you true?"

"It's all BS and rumors," he said.

He liked to drink a lot, but it never appeared to be a problem. His personality didn't change causing him to become violent or aggressive from what I observed.

One night we were at the club playing darts and hanging out with friends. We were getting along well, and everyone was having fun. The evening was winding down, and people were leaving.

"You wanna go back to my barracks room to watch a movie and hang out some more?" he asked me.

"Sure." I walked with him the short distance. I towed behind him down the hallway to his room to watch *A Time to Kill* on the television. The closer we got, the more he talked about sex. Contrary to my high-school boyfriend calling me a whore, I was still a virgin.

"I'm not going to have sex with you," I stated numerous times. I didn't think much about our conversation as I crossed over the threshold into his control.

I blamed myself for everything

"Come now, let's settle this," says the LORD. "Though your sins are like scarlet, I will make them as white as snow. Though they are red like crimson, I will make them as white as wool."

Isaiah 1:18 (NLT)

"Did I just get raped?" I asked myself out loud while I drove home later that night. I knew the story of Genesis 19:4-5. What the men of Sodom in Lot's village wanted to do to the visiting angel had just happened to me. I shivered as I remembered James telling me, "It's okay. You'll still be a virgin if we do it this way."

I couldn't believe someone could be so determined and abrasive. I had squirmed and pulled myself forward to get away. I knocked over his stack of books at the end of the bed and his makeshift nightstand in my attempt to stop what was happening.

My memories tried to make sense of it all. It was like reading a page out of a book that told of unspeakable horrors to only realize I'd written it.

If I questioned whether or not I'd imagined everything, the marks on my body confirmed my fears. I had bruises and scratches along the inside and outside of my thighs and on my stomach. Every time I'd tried to move away or in a different direction, he'd pulled me back. There was also the bleeding. I was too afraid to do anything about it.

"You need to go to the hospital," my friend Angela told me. That night I confided in her what happened. She did not agree that I should simply curl up in a ball and will my physical damage to go away.

She made an appointment at the hospital for me and told them it was because I was raped. I reluctantly saw a doctor. I felt like I was a young child again, resuffering the trauma that happened after I was abducted out of my bedroom. I wasn't allowed to leave the hospital for over five hours. Only after I talked to the Army Criminal Investigation Division did I go home.

At first, I did everything I could to tell James what was going on.

"I promise I won't say anything," I told him in person after I was released from the hospital. "I'm so sorry this is happening. I never wanted this."

"I blacked out," he said. "I don't remember anything from last night." He placed his hands over his face and rubbed up and down, over and over. His eyes looked up toward the ceiling as if it had answers written across it. I could tell he was stressing about it.

I told him everything that happened.

"Did I hit you?" He was looking right at me then. I stared at him in disbelief. He just confirmed every word of caution I was told. *The rumors are true. I'm so lucky it wasn't worse than what it could've been.*

"You were very physical. I have marks on my body."
I broke eye contact for a moment. He didn't say anything, so I glanced back up at him. "We can work
through it. I don't want to report anything."

I blamed myself for everything and tried to "fix"
things with him many times. I hated myself. I thought
I caused this and seemed to completely forget what he
had done to me. I never asked for the abuse. I figured
somehow the rape was my fault. I wanted to light a fire
to the bad memories. *Would I ever meet someone who
would care for me and love me unconditionally like my
father? Would the abuse ever stop?*

I curled up on my bed after I heard James was telling
people he wished I were dead. My hair was disheveled,
and my pale face rivaled Michelangelo's statue of *David*.
The glow from the television was the only light in the
room. I couldn't hear the actor's conversation over my
many thoughts that sounded like a swarm of bees.

I stood in front of my mirror in my barracks room
and literally punched myself in the face over and over.
James wanted me dead. I thought everything was my
fault, and this was my way of forcing me to pay for it.
They sent me to Germany. I was put in the psych ward
for a week. They thought I was not cooperating with
the investigation because I was afraid of James. I wasn't
cooperating because I never wanted to report it in the
first place. I blamed myself.

We'd had our last friendly conversation when I
spoke to him face-to-face before my time in Germany.
Shortly after that, his leadership told him to stay away
from me. His entire attitude changed. He told people

he wanted to kill me for ruining his career. He also made snide comments about a domestic violence issue if I got near him.

That was when I became afraid of him. The panic I always felt when I worried about losing my father compounded with the notions of James ending my life. Any time I saw him or his friends, I was given this death stare. When I was around base by myself, I felt so uncomfortable. Therefore, I stopped going places alone. I would drag my friends everywhere.

After a week in the psych ward in Germany, I began drinking like a fish. I often showed up to work drunk and drank until I passed out every weekend. I didn't want to think about it, and I wanted to forget what was going on. I wanted the alcohol to bring warm, fuzzy feelings to replace my racing heart.

I was a total mess, but I thought I was okay and in control. I would brag to my friends about how much I could drink for such a small person and how I threw up almost every color possible. The next year passed by in an inebriated blur.

I was in counseling. They warned against me starting a relationship with anyone. "You have a lot of issues you need to work through first."

Of course I didn't listen. In fact, that just added fuel to the fire. I tried to fast track my healing and wanted to prove I *was* healthy enough to date. I started a relationship with another MP, Zack, and tried to clean up my act. I went back to church. My new boyfriend was very good looking with brown hair and eyes. What I cherished most about him was that he was a Christian.

I loved him, and he was a good guy and treated me well. But I was forcing things to prove I was okay.

We talked about getting married, and I let everything go. I lost my virginity to him at the age of twenty-one because we were talking about marriage. I thought, *That makes it okay, right?* He was the first *good* person who actually loved me and wanted to be with me forever. When he went back to the states, we fell further apart. We fought like crazy. It wasn't over a lot of things, but one of the big issues was James. I was obsessed with fixing that relationship. I couldn't stand the thought of him hating me or talking about wanting me dead. Zack refused to deal with it. After he was back in the states, he said he couldn't trust me. So we called it off.

I was like a chameleon. I really had no idea who I was or what I needed. I learned through my abuse to be what the other person wanted. I didn't like myself, which made learning who I was a tough assignment. If I couldn't have a productive relationship with myself, I couldn't expect to have one with someone else.

Another tailspin happened at that point. The drinking got worse. I figured since I threw my virginity away I should just keep going. So I started sleeping around for attention.

I could hear God telling me, "Come back to me." I think that made me sprint in the opposite direction. I was my own worst critic. I told myself what everyone else in my life said to me. I thought, *I am a horrible person who doesn't deserve anything good. I am a whore and worthless.* I slept with three people that year and tried to act like I was okay with it, but it tore me apart inside.

I had waited so long with every intention of waiting until I was married and threw it all away. I hated myself for that. I tried to abuse myself by all of the drinking and stupidity I was doing. The guilt I felt from sleeping around and drinking myself into oblivion was more than I could handle.

I almost broke up a marriage that year. I became friends with a guy, and we got along really well. I actually felt safe around him, unlike most of the men around me.

We hung out at the softball games, base club, and I even took him to the strip club in Antwerp with some other male friends. It was the first time I had been to a strip club, but it was fun to mess with the guys. We talked about everything from work to trouble in his marriage. It snowballed from there, and we both knew we were in too deep.

Even though I didn't like his wife, I never intended for something to happen. I never wanted to hurt anyone. I just got tunnel vision and forgot the other details.

Although we never had sex, we went way too far. He gave me more reasons to hate myself and believe everything I had been told over the years. His wife found out, and our friendship blew up. I didn't care for his wife and tried to find every reason to justify what happened. But inside I knew it was wrong. I knew I was just running farther from God.

Furthermore, I would tell myself that God could never want someone like me. I knew he loved me and would forgive me, but I couldn't shake my guilt. I told myself the lies many people do: *God will never forgive me for what I've done. Sexual immorality is the worst, and it's against God.* I continued to belittle myself constantly.

In January of 2001, I took a trip to see my Navy SEAL. I had a huge crush on Ryan while we were deployed in Kuwait. I wanted him to be my boyfriend, but I knew he didn't see me that way. So I settled for having him like a big brother. He always looked out for me and was there when I needed someone to talk to or just vent with.

I took leave to go to Norfolk, Virginia, and spent a week with my friend, Ryan. He was a sweetheart and just as adorable as when I saw him three years earlier. We had a good time hanging out, and it started off as a great trip. He had a roommate named Kevin. He was a former Navy SEAL as well but was very cocky.

We all went out to a club one night, and of course I had a lot to drink. We got back to the apartment. I'm not sure what happened to my friend, but I ended up in his roommate's room.

Kevin sexually assaulted me and then threw me out of his room after he saw my face covered in tears. I went to the bathroom to clean up and then went to bed in my friend's room. I never told Ryan what happened. I always blamed myself and told myself I asked for it. Ryan could tell something was different though. I became distant for the remainder of the visit. That was the way I handled things, though. I just shut down and kept on going through life to survive.

I became an expert at building walls around myself and bottling up my emotions and feelings. Occasionally I would explode, usually by myself. I became great at acting like I didn't care around others.

The summer of 2001 was a great time, though. Two of my best friends and I traveled Germany with a USO band and had an absolute blast! Connie, Gini, and I ran away that summer traveling through Germany and Austria. Gini was a tomboy version of a country girl with dark-brown hair. We were like the gals from *Sex and the City*. We just let loose and were living carefree!

Connie, Gini, & Me

We made wonderful friends with the band members and saw gorgeous parts of that amazing country. I was trying to get my life back on track by becoming more involved in church and not drinking heavily. I knew I was separating from the air force in August and going home to live with Dad for a little while. I had to get myself right because I could not go home a mess. I couldn't let my dad see me that way. I was too ashamed and embarrassed. I never wanted to disappoint him.

I separated from the air force in August of 2001 after my four-year requirement was fulfilled. They wanted to send me to Minot, North Dakota. This Texas girl said, "No, thank you!" I went home.

Dad and me after I left the Air Force 2001

Then September 11, 2001 happened. My dad woke me up. "You need to come see the news."

This was one of those moments that you never forget where you were when it happened. I remember sitting on the ottoman in the living room thinking, *Is this real? Is this actually happening in our country?* I decided to wait and see if I was going to get called back before I started college. I had no idea if we were going to war or what this would really mean. But I knew there was a chance I could be required to go back to active duty.

I never got a call to go back, so I began attending community college and looked at ROTC (Reserve Officer Training Corps) programs. I voluntarily served my country when we weren't at war, and I knew that I had to go back and do my part after they attacked my country.

I decided I needed to get my life right with God. I started attending church services and cracked open a Bible. In January of 2002, I began community college close to home so I could stay with Dad. I needed my "north star" to keep me grounded for a while. Daddy didn't know it, but he helped me slow down my spiral of destruction and get back in touch with God.

The following year I got my associate of arts degree. Then I moved to Denton, Texas, to attend the University of North Texas on a ROTC scholarship. I studied criminal justice.

One of the first days of ROTC, I saw a guy walk in. I thought, *He's gorgeous. I want to meet him.* Initially it was difficult. Steven was a cross-town student, meaning he attended another school but attended ROTC classes with us. We met and chatted a few times. Eventually one of my friends set it up for us to hang out on my birthday. Our group ate out, and he was there.

The relationship grew from there. We officially began dating on December 24, 2003. It appeared he had his life together. It all seemed too good to be true. Well, you know what they say about that. If it seems too good to be true, then it probably is.

He quickly won over the majority of the people close to me with his charm. SSgt Manners from ROTC tried to warn me from the beginning this was a bad move. He kept telling me not to fall for it and to walk away. I didn't listen.

I was so afraid I'd never find someone who would want to be with me and actually marry me. I had done so many awful things I didn't believe anyone could truly love me and want to be with me forever. Therefore, when he said he wanted to marry me, I ran with it. I had reservations, but most of the people around me highly approved of him. No one really raised any concerns, so I thought it had to be right.

I never told Steven everything about my past. I told him a few things about being molested and physically abused, but I never let him in completely. Those were my skeletons, and I didn't want to share.

One day I went to his apartment. As I started walking up the stairs, I saw rose petals. I knew what was coming, but I wasn't excited. I'm not sure what I felt. It wasn't fear, but it wasn't anything you'd expect someone to feel when she knows she's about to be proposed to.

I opened the door, and he was in the middle of rose petals in the shape of a heart on one knee. As he asked me to marry him, I had a million thoughts in my head. There were no tears of joy, and I felt like I should say no, but I didn't. I said yes, with many reservations in my heart.

Daddy & Me

We got married exactly one year after we started dating. Things slowly changed. His parents paid for everything he had before we got married but stopped after. It was a huge adjustment for him, but his spending didn't stop. His parents started telling us what we were going to name our kids and just stepping over boundaries.

His mom and I quickly started to clash. She liked being in control of everything, and I wasn't going to allow that to happen. Between money issues and his parents, I was getting fed up quickly. It came to a head when his family took us to Washington, DC, for Christmas in 2005 over our one-year anniversary.

We went to dinner at a very nice restaurant and then took a taxi back to the hotel. Besides our chauffer, there was my husband and myself, his parents, and his niece in the car. The foreign driver was on the phone while driving us back to the hotel.

"Can you believe this?" Steven's mother remarked in a disapproving tone. "Excuse me, driver. Driver, do *you* mind?" She talked down to him like he was a three-year-old who'd just been caught licking the birthday cake.

"How idiotic can you be? Don't you know how dangerous it is to talk on the phone and drive? You must be new at this."

I was mortified and could not believe she was being so rude about it. She couldn't just let him know that she would prefer him to not be on the phone. No, she had to put him down and belittle him the entire ride back to the hotel. When we arrived and began getting out of the vehicle, I and his eleven-year-old niece apologized for the woman's actions. I told my husband that was beyond inappropriate. When a pre-teen is embarrassed, it is obviously not okay.

"Sir, I'm so sorry about that," I said to him through the rolled-down front passenger window. I could not say sorry enough times. His mom knew I apologized to the driver and started yelling at me as we went into the elevator.

"Tiffany, how rude of you. I was completely in the right, and our driver was completely in the wrong. I don't want you apologizing for something that you should've said in the first place."

"How could you talk to the man like that?" I began. As the elevator went to the higher levels, my rage rose with it. "I am completely offended by how you treated him."

That just threw her into a rage. Her eyes narrowed, and she slightly lowered her head. She looked like a finely manicured bull about to charge.

We got off the elevator. I started walking toward Steven's and my room.

"Son, come here," she said in a commanding voice. I didn't even slow my pace down. I opened the door and then plopped down on the queen-sized bed and stared at the black television screen. I didn't want to turn it on. What I wanted was to slap my mother-in-law across the face. *Doesn't she care at all about other people's feelings? I sure don't want her talking to me that way.*

She was so loud I could hear her say, "You know, you don't have to be married to her forever!" Maybe she made sure to say it loud enough for me to catch that first sentence. The rest of their conversation wasn't as easy to discern.

Neither of his parents spoke to me for the remainder of the trip. That included our flight home and the drive to our apartment. A couple of days later I told my husband that I was fed up.

"Between your parents and our financial situation, I can't handle it anymore. You need to get a job and stop blowing all our money." We both cried. He promised to find work and change things. By this time, he'd gone through three vehicles while we were together, all on my credit. I had to get a $25,000 loan because we ran through my savings. The money coming in wasn't enough.

Things didn't change. After the new year came, we moved in with my dad because I couldn't pay all the bills anymore. This meant an hour-and-a-half drive for me to school daily. I couldn't handle the bills alone anymore or the spending habits. I felt like a failure for moving in with my father at that stage of my life, but I didn't have any other alternative.

Months went by, and things were not any different. I was losing respect for my husband daily. My Prince Charming was turning into a frog instead of the other way around. It had gotten to the point where when he kissed me I was repulsed. My body quivered when he walked away. I knew with the way I felt I had to just call it quits.

In May 2006, I filed for divorce. I immediately started paying off the debt. It was nearly $50,000. I took all the bills and just walked away, leaving him with his Harley as the only consolation. Everything was in my name, and I couldn't make sure he would shell out for them.

His mom went back and forth about our divorce. For months she was telling him he didn't have to be with me and to separate from me. Then when I filed, she called Steven and made the craziest statement I have ever heard a parent say to their child: "If she is divorcing you, then so are we!"

I have no idea why, but the woman was all over the place. Then after she saw how hurt he was, she changed her tune and came after me. She tried to say I was leaving because I cheated on him. She threatened to sue me. I gave him the furniture he wanted—the demand that came with that threat just to make them go away. His parents wanted to control everything in his life, and I refused to be part of it.

I loved him, but I chose to marry him out of the fears my abusive past had created. I worried, *Will anyone want to marry me?* I didn't feel worthy of a loving relationship. I felt a ton of guilt for getting divorced and stopped going to church, too. *How could God smile down on me while I listened to the pastor preach after what I'd done?*

That month I also graduated and commissioned in the air force as an officer as a second lieutenant. I asked Col Hull, whom I met on my first deployment to Kuwait, to come and commission me. He happily accepted and flew into DFW May 13, 2006 to commission me as a second lieutenant in the United States Air Force. I was so honored to have him as my commissioning officer.

Steven's and my divorce was final by July 10. By October I was stationed in Mountain Home, Idaho. I looked forward to the new start. His parents were not done trying to control my life though.

Shortly after I arrived, I was sent to school in Ohio for almost six weeks on a TDY. My now ex-husband's parents started calling my commander.

"That woman is a horrible person. We can't believe the air force has people in it like her." They threatened my commander. "We're going to the press if something isn't done to get her out."

I could not believe they had gone to such lengths to harass me. Thankfully, the commander called me to discuss things instead of just taking their word for it. Nothing was done, and I moved on.

Kris, Kevin, Me and David

My second deployment began in January of 2007, lasting four months. I was stationed in Balad, Iraq. Initially, I was so excited because of the group I was going with. At first we were a strong team, but things changed shortly after getting into the country.

"You are worthless and piss poor at everything," my new commander, whom I called Satan's Spawn, told me almost daily.

hawaiian coconut coffee and falling in love

So he got up and went to his father. "But while he was still a long way off, his father saw him and was filled with compassion for him; he ran to his son, threw his arms around him and kissed him. The son said to him, 'Father, I have sinned against heaven and against you. I am no longer worthy to be called your son.' But the father said to his servants, 'For this son of mine was dead and is alive again; he was lost and is found.' So they began to celebrate."

Luke 15:20-22a, 24 (NIV)

Satan's Spawn made it very clear that he would get me out of the air force if he could. He implied in a not-so-subtle way that I was a slut. He also said, "Every decision you make is wrong."

After getting tired of hearing this week after week, I snapped back. "I decided to go to the restroom earlier, and it was a good decision." I know it wasn't appropriate, but I was fed up with being torn apart and just taking it.

"*When* you get caught sleeping around, I will take you down and get you kicked out of the air force." The overweight, short man was about a foot away from me when he said that.

I lost it. I replied, "I don't care about your rank. You will *not* imply that I'm a slut and get away with it." It was frightening, but it felt so good finally standing up for myself.

I went to MEO (Military Equal Opportunity Office) multiple times and to the group commander. No one ever did anything. I had to just suck it up and deal with it daily. Usually I got feedback once or twice a year from a supervisor. He gave me hateful feedback weekly.

I'd never experienced someone intentionally trying to break me apart like that. It was awful working for a man who thrived on demeaning others to make himself feel better. It was unbelievable to me this man had a psychology degree!

Satan's Spawn went after my enlisted troops as well. I wasn't even given the chance to defend them or provide any top cover. I was more concerned about the people doing the mission working for me than getting myself awards or personal kudos. Many of my subordinates told me they always knew I had their backs and would fight for them if they were right.

"I would follow you into battle any day or go to war with you any time," I heard regularly. It's always about the team, not me. I've been told that would be my downfall as an officer, but I don't agree. I believe that is my strength. Without our enlisted troops, the mission wouldn't get done. If you don't take care of them, they won't do their best for you.

I didn't handle the stress well at all. Working out daily was not helping me. I tried to talk to friends I had made while I was there. That just amounted to venting and nothing more. I tried to figure out what I needed to do to make my commander happy.

It wasn't like I just sat on my butt all day and never did anything, but what I was doing was never good enough for him. It was so frustrating. He wasn't giving me constructive guidance. Instead he just criticized.

Working for that man was identical to being in an abusive relationship. I felt as though I couldn't get away, and I had to deal with it. The only difference was there was no physical relationship, no chemistry. Like most abusive people I've encountered, he took every opportunity to attack me. He made sure no one was around to witness it.

Dealing with my commander was just as difficult an issue as abuse. This was being attacked on a personal *and* professional level though. He didn't just tell me I wasn't a good officer; he told me I sucked as a person too. I guess in some ways experiencing previous abuses prepared me to deal with him, but every unhealthy encounter was unique.

On top of this frustration I still had horrible guilt from my divorce. I didn't feel like I deserved God's love and forgiveness…even though I knew he had already given it to me. I wasn't able to cry out to my heavenly Father or read the Bible for encouragement to get me through this conflict. I was like a soldier on a spiritual battlefield trying to fight without a shield or any weapons.

When I returned home from my deployment, I started drinking and acting out again. I was engaging in abusive ways and spending time with the wrong guys again. I was allowing them to control me and treat me like a piece of meat. The Commander I hated left about two months after we returned. He made sure to tell the incoming Commander that I was horrible and would self-implode within months.

Daddy & Me

I really liked the new commander, Major James. I'd soon learn he was a great leader and mentor. I took advantage of getting a new chance to prove myself. I was still getting drunk and partying on the weekends to relieve stress. However, at work I was doing my best to show I was a good airman.

I was a food service officer and did everything I could to get my team to be number one in the air force. I knew we would be competing for the Hennessy Award. I wanted my great team to win because they worked hard. We started ramping up. Two months before we were going to be inspected, we were kicking butt. I scrutinized them weekly on every checklist item necessary. I worked twelve to fourteen-hour days to make sure we had all bases covered.

The time to shine arrived. I told them before everything started, "You deserve this because you have been doing your absolute best for months." They knew what was expected, and they wanted to excel. Every fiber of my body wanted them to come first.

Our team exceeded in everything! I bit my lip as I impatiently waited to be notified who the winners were. We all gathered in the dining facility where my commander and the wing commander would announce who would be the victor.

"Your team is the winner of the John L. Hennessy Award for Best Air Force Multiple Facilities." They were both looking right at me. I burst into tears. The squadron commander was crying and the airmen were cheering. It was awesome. I finally felt like I was part of something good and had contributed positively to something.

I thought back on when Major James called me into his office and told me the previous commander's doubts about me. I was so happy to not only prove

Satan's Spawn wrong but be part of the team that won the highest food service award in the air force!

In spite of the victory, I was still drinking and crying for attention in all the wrong ways. It was slowly getting better though. Winning that award helped tremendously. While we were TDY to Chicago, Illinois, to receive our trophy, I was notified my next deployment was changed.

During the phone conversation, I was told, "You will be leaving in two weeks for army CST (combat skills training) then deploying to Afghanistan for six months." That involved being in Ft. Riley, Kansas, June through August.

That wasn't where I was supposed to go initially. Originally I was scheduled to head to the UAE (United Arab Emirates in the Middle East) in September 2008 for four months. This *would've* been my first deployment I wouldn't be shot at or have people attempting to blow me up.

I decided then I needed to get myself back on track and in line with God's will for my life. It was time to start living the way he and I knew I should. I felt so far away, and I needed to focus on him. To do that, I planned on going to church, praying often, and reading my Bible.

I wanted my heart to burn with love like it had when I prayed for God to comfort Charley after I couldn't tell him good-bye in junior high. Days before leaving, I rested my head on my pillow and prayed as I drifted off to sleep. *God, let me be close to you. Wrap your arms around me, and fill me with your love.*

The training in Kansas was useful. The only frustrating part was doing things the army way instead of how I'm used to the air force doing it. In August of 2008, I began my third deployment.

After arriving in Kabul, Afghanistan, I settled into a comfortable routine. Part of that involved mentoring the Afghan National Army (ANA). At the same time, there were other military members mentoring the Afghan National Police (ANP). It's one thing to be on base doing my job. It's completely different to interact with the locals. Seeing how they live was an eye-opening experience. We convoyed from our base to the ANA Logistics Command (LOG CMD) compound.

Ready to Convoy

I wrote many e-mails home to family and friends discussing how everything was affecting me. Since I was born and raised in America, I couldn't imagine how a third-world country lived. Only after experiencing it firsthand did my heart break. I saw how poverty-stricken children lived and how jubilantly they acted when given toys.

From: Tiffany
Date: October 2, 2008
To: All my friends

Hello all,

I thought enough time had passed for me to send another update for everyone. My ankle is getting better for all of you that keep asking. The pretty colors are all gone, but it is still a little tender if turned the wrong way. When I'm all better, I'll start working out and running like I need to. I had a small taste of food poisoning or I guess you could say coffee poisoning. That wasn't any fun. When that subsided, the allergies moved in to complicate things. So things seem to just keep rolling. This isn't shaping up to be my best deployment, but I'm alive and can keep in touch with all of you, so I will be happy about that.

As for my job, things are slowly moving along. I'm getting used to going outside the wire now. Don't think I mean I like it by any means, but it is becoming a routine for me. The intent of my job is to advise/mentor the ANA (Afghan National Army) DFAC (dining facility) managers. I have to use an interpreter to have conversations, which slows things down, but it's a learning process for all of us. I figure it will push me a little harder to learn the language and better myself at the same time.

Just to give you an idea of what I have ahead of me, they are used to cooking all of their meals by wood. Seriously, without sounding rude, think caveman times almost. I feel bad because we are almost trying to move an entire country from way back then to today without any steps in between. It is very hard for them to understand using propane in the kitchen. They don't understand they will have fire without smoke burning their eyes. It is truly hard for us to grasp how poor this country is. I'm here, and I can hardly grasp it myself. I promise to send pictures when I can though.

Last week I also went out on a humanitarian mission. We took clothes, kites, soccer balls, school supplies, and tons of other stuff out to a local village. That was an experience I will never forget. I will attach pictures of that soon as well. I don't have the means to right now though. These kids don't have much of anything, and any time we handed something to one, they would all start fighting and knocking each other over to take it. I've never seen children act this way, nor can I imagine what they must feel when they see us show up with all of the gifts and stuff we have.

I would love to write a story and have it published in a local newspaper or run on the local news at home so people could see what we are doing here. Our mission is the hearts and minds of the people here, not war and killing like many think. It is truly sad how many people are just ignorant to what the military does in general, much less over here. I don't want to get on my soapbox though.

I pray that you are happy to hear actual details of what I'm doing. I don't have all the time I would like to write this and tell you everything, but I do try. God and I have been a little distant since my divorce, but that is one thing I'm truly determined to straighten up while I'm here. I pray that between the mission work and my job I get to see many miracles he can do in this country. I'm blessed to be able to be a part of the mission we are doing. It could truly almost be missionaries doing this instead, but no, this is what the US Armed Forces are doing for our country and theirs.

We are dedicated to helping this nation stand on its own. Maybe if you learn nothing about what the military does from my e-mails you'll learn that pulling us out of here all at once will truly destroy this nation that has been at war for decades. All they want is a fighting chance, and they are so happy we are here to help and work to rebuild and better their nation.

Okay, I guess I got on my soapbox a little, but now you know my heart, and if you want to discuss or argue, that is your right.

Home of the free because of the brave!

Tiffany Dawn

In addition to spending time writing e-mails, I worked on my relationship with God. I felt good about myself the more I filled my time with spiritual activities. I wanted to know God's deep love for me. I'd read about how he was close to the broken hearted and treated the wounded with gentleness. My heart was like a broken mirror with shards of glass scattered across the floor. Because of the shattering experiences, I ached to be held like a lamb in the Shepherd's arms. I knew God wanted to put all the pieces back together to reflect his glory.

In order to experience that, I thought it'd be best to keep any potential datable males farther than an arm's length. Then one day Gabe walked into the office. His slender frame was six feet tall, he had blond hair and baby-blue eyes.

I prayed a hundred times that nothing would happen with us. I thought of "Daughters of Jerusalem, I charge you by the gazelles and by the does of the field: Do not arouse or awaken love until it so desires," (Song of Solomon 2:7, NIV).

This couldn't be the time God would bring the man he desires to be my husband into my life, could it? I struggled with my feelings. Gabe was amazing, but I told God I wasn't ready. I needed to focus on him alone. I begged for him to take any interest and attraction away because I knew it wasn't good for me. It didn't work. God had another plan for us. I wasn't trying to awaken love, but it seemed like God was.

As time progressed, I felt things change in my heart. Gabe and I sat outside of the church tent one night and talked for hours. I barely noticed the slight taste of sand in my mouth that was typical for our location. I wanted to keep the stars from forming above in an attempt to stop time. We were so wrapped up in our conversation we missed the service going on inside.

"So tell me about your father," he said. His eyes stared intently into mine like he was trying to see the answers to his questions swimming around in them.

I took a deep breath and glanced up. Images of my dad flashed across my mind like shuffling loose photos. I stopped on one of us at Christmas time when I was just a little kid. There was wrapping paper littering the floor all around us.

My mom took the picture. Thinking about it made me wonder what she was up to. I barely spoke to her even this long after my parents went through their divorce.

"He's my hero," I replied, not letting the seeds of wonder about my mother take root in the soil of my heart. I shared about my life growing up. After talking nonstop for three minutes, I blushed then looked down.

"I think I've been doing all the talking. Tell me about your family."

Gabe discussed the Christian family he grew up in. As he spoke, I marveled about how he was different from everyone else. He wasn't like all the other guys in my life before. Maybe that's what caught my attention. Even though he was smart and well educated, if a coworker praised his intelligence, he downplayed the information he'd shared.

"I'm a Christian and want to live in God's will," he said after he finished sharing about his upbringing.

Cupid's arrows were hitting my heart. But I continued to pray that God would burn them up. I wasn't over the guilt of my divorce and didn't want to get married again.

I felt as though God said, "Just hold on and trust me." I gripped the love of God like a ten-year-old clinging to the bar in front of him on a roller coaster. *How would I survive getting flung off this ride if Gabe and I fell in love but it didn't work out?*

When I finally stopped fighting my emotions, I knew Cupid didn't need any more arrows. I started writing to my dad, informing him about this amazing man I had met. He e-mailed me back to let me know he was excited for me.

My daddy and I e-mailed back and forth often.

> From: donc1@att.blackberry.net
> Date: October 29, 2008 4:28:23 AM
> GMT-07:00
> To: "Tiff"
> Subject: Re: I'm done...
>
> U go girl! Me and the girls think it is wonderful. Since Gabe makes you feel this way, then I am for you all the way. Having a Christian-based faith will make your relationship stronger. All I want to say is be happy, enjoy each other. May God bless you both and keep y'all safe. Love you always. Daddy

Gabe was exactly who my father would have picked for me if one thousand men stood side by side in a lineup. I'd found the love of my life and couldn't be happier. Sleeping Beauty had just woken up to discover her prince. I hoped we would have the happily-ever-after, fairy-tale ending.

Then I started letting my best friends and family know about Gabe and how wonderful he was.

From: Tiffany
Date: Wed, 29 Oct 2008
To: My Friends
Subject: I'm done…

This is it. You may have to hold me to it, but I'm done… I don't want anyone else. I want to work as hard as I need to make this relationship work for the rest of my life! I said it. You can shut your mouth now and take a breath! I haven't felt this way in *so* long, and I'm gonna enjoy every minute of it! So kick me in the backside if I ever say otherwise and bring me to my senses. I *love* Gabe, and I want to have his babies! I pray none of you are having heart attacks right now! Haha!

Seriously, I am so happy, and I can't believe I feel this way. I thought after my divorce I was done. I closed off my heart and didn't want another serious relationship…*ever*! God is a true miracle worker. I can't believe what he has done for me and in my life since I've been here. I can't believe I had to come all the stinking way to Afghanistan to become this person either.

I've never thought, *I want to put everything I have into this relationship.* I will work as hard as I need to make this work and make him happy. He makes me so happy and keeps me laughing all the time. It's just so easy to be with him, and it scares the crap out of me—but I don't care. I want this, and it blows my mind!

His parents are awesome. They've been e-mailing me, and what a blessing it is to know as in-laws they won't drive me to the crazy house! They are sweet-spirited Christians and so friendly.

I know you are probably in shock, and you may have a thousand questions. Well, you aren't alone. I have plenty of scary moments. I can't believe I feel this way every day. I have thousands of questions I ask Gabe all the time. More importantly, I ask God how this is possible and thank him every day and all day long for all of this and for all of you!

Please write whenever you want/can and tell me what you think or what questions you want to ask... I'm *so* happy!

He reminded me of Dad. It wasn't about the big, flashy stuff. Instead it was about the little things. There wasn't anything over the top. He was content just talking, drinking coffee, hiking, or watching a movie.

I felt God leading me to him no matter how hard I fought. Only two weeks after becoming an official couple into the dating part of our relationship, I could not believe the feelings I had for him or that they came so fast and hard. For the first time in my life, I wanted to tell someone I loved them before they told me. After Paul shared of his love for me in less than a month of our time together, I replied that he was crazy. This was completely different for me, and I knew it was all God.

Gabe made us Hawaiian coconut coffee every morning. We sat and chatted for ten to fifteen minutes before having to separate. He woke up early for our dates because he convoyed to work later than I did. It was the most thoughtful thing a guy had done for me. We even read the Bible together daily.

He won my heart. I really never had a chance. I knew God orchestrated this relationship. He changed my deployment, which brought me to another part of the world. Here I met Gabe. It was a love story filled with danger though. We were around the threat of death daily. I prayed for Gabe constantly because of that.

God, don't let me screw this up

The troubles of my heart have multiplied; free
me from my anguish.

Psalm 25:17 (NIV)

We couldn't date like usual people since we were
always worried about our lives. But we made it work.
We watched movies together in the library or on our
laptops. Our ritual of coffee in the morning continued as the weeks passed. Sometimes we played cards
with friends.

If Gabe saw pecan pie at one of the dining facilities
he convoyed to, he would bring it back to me. It was
something I loved. He never missed an opportunity
to show he cared. We worked out together when we
could. Once a week we went to the Thai food restaurant on base for date night.

We talked about everything you could imagine,
from religion to finances to kids. It amazed me how
much we agreed on. I admired and respected him more
than any guy in my life before, except my daddy, of
course. Gabe was the first man who could measure up
and who treated me like my dad always told me a gentleman should.

We went to church together, and it all felt like God's plan. The simplest touch to my back or arm made me feel safe. I wanted everything to be different about this dating relationship. I started praying, "God, don't let me screw this up."

I decided I needed to be honest about my past and what I had been through. Not just some of it, either. I wanted to tell him everything so he would know that I wasn't perfect and what abuse I'd suffered. I wanted to be seen as honest in his eyes. He seemed to do well with the information. The only problem was he was raised in such a perfect world he couldn't truly understand what I had been through.

His parents protected him from everything. He never experienced any abuse, neglect, trauma, or anything along those lines. The worst thing he went through was loved ones dying. That is a part of life, and everyone goes through that, but not abuse, murder, or abandonment. I know he sympathized, but that wasn't enough. He needed to comprehend the damage my past caused.

Everything wasn't perfect. We had a few disagreements like all couples do. This relationship was special though, so I did my best to express how I felt. I'd never done that before. In the past, I used the silent treatment when my heart felt bruised. When we would have a disagreement, my heart would literally hurt. I had never experienced that before. I was good at shutting down. But I didn't want it to be that way with Gabe. I wanted to make this work because I knew God had brought us together.

In spite of my feelings for Gabe, I knew I was on a deployment and made sure to focus on safety. I paid attention to the news. I e-mailed my daddy about one event.

From: Tiffany
Date: Thu, 27 Nov 2008
To: Don
Subject: Kabul attack

In case you hear about the attack on the news, I forgot to tell you on the phone. We had a suicide car bomber blow himself up about 600 yards outside of base this morning. It killed 4 local nationals and wounded about 17 more. No US troops or coalition troops were around, thankfully. People felt it shake on base about 0845, and Daryl told me after it happen when he heard the news. I was in bed watching *House* on my computer. So don't worry about me; we are good. I just wanted to make sure to tell you about it from my end versus what you would hear on the news. I love you and miss you bunches. God bless y'all and keep y'all safe always.

My father e-mailed me back.

From: don
Date: November 27, 2008
To: "Tiff"
Subject: Re: Kabul attack

I did get to see a news clip on the Kabul attack. The story I was most interested in was a mission like you go on. They took medical supplies and other things to a village. The kids needed food and medicine. My thoughts were, *This is what my baby girl is doing.* My heart filled with pride. I could not be more proud of you. I wish that more people could see the good that you all are doing over there. It is something else that I am thankful for, being your father. Have a great day. Hi to Gabe. Love you always. Daddy

I tried my best to update my friends back in America what was going on with my life while deployed. I sent them this e-mail two weeks before Christmas.

Afghan girl and me

From: Tiff
Date: Dec 13, 2008
To: My Friends
Subject: Update

Hello all,

I know my updates have drifted off lately, and I'm sorry for that. My master's class is kicking my butt in all honesty. I thought it would be easy to study terrorism while I'm in this country. What was I thinking? Ha!

Okay, since the last e-mail I have only been on one trip, non-work related. We haven't been allowed off base too much since the threat level is going up. Joy! My last trip was to a maternity ward. Ladies, be grateful for whatever you had and/or have in the future when you give birth. These women were two to a bed—yes, that is what you read. They had about seven beds or so to a room, and this was before and after giving birth. Keeping in mind this country is beyond poor in American standards, they have people separated by status.

The very poor village women were in a completely different part of the building from the rest of the women. The premature babies were in their own room, but they had four babies to one baby bed. Yes, the typical bed your baby is in had four babies nearly stacked in the same bed. It is beyond belief the things you see here. Now don't think it is because the people are just uncivilized or something. That isn't it at all. Unfortunately, it is simply because they don't have the capability to do better for their own people. These are the reasons we are here. We are trying to better this country daily by giving them the knowledge and items needed to do better for themselves. If given the chance and means to rebuild this country, they will learn what it is like to have a good life and education.

The shock and sadness I've experienced in this country will be with me for the rest of my life. I wish there was a way I could get the message out to more people. We aren't here to kill people and blow things up. We are here to rebuild a nation that has longed to stand on its own two feet but have never been allowed to. We are not here to occupy a country or make them do things the "American" way. We are here to give a country a fighting chance to survive on its own.

I promise not to get on my soapbox today, so this will be shorter than most. Ha! I pray you enjoy hearing a different side of what the US and coalition forces are doing over here. I'm pretty sure CNN isn't running stories like this.

Have a great day, and don't take for granted what God has provided to you and your family in the free country you *choose* to live in!

God bless y'all and keep y'all safe always.

The next e-mail I sent related to a conversation I had with a coworker.

My Afghan General, his Deputy and me in Kabul, Afghanistan

From: Tiffany
Date: Sun, 4 Jan 2009
To: My Friends
Subject: Afghan small update...

Hello all,

Yesterday my general asked me a tough question I wasn't expecting! He reminded me that seven years ago we ran the Taliban out and there were no suicide bombers or anything for years. Then he proceeded to ask, Why are they back now? Wow, talk about a blow to the kidney! All I could say was that our current focus, from my understanding, were the "hearts and minds" of the local nationals. In the last month, we've even been told to tone down our aggressive driving and blend in.

I said I couldn't speak for the coalition forces. He then wanted to know if Obama would actually do what he said now that he was in office. "Obama said he would eradicate the Taliban," and the people want to know if that is really going to happen. What is different now than in 2001 when we ran them out? Have we gone soft? It crushed me to look at him and not have an answer to that all-important question. These people are tired of war, and they want peace! He said he would like to see peace before he dies. I tried to explain that this wasn't going to be a quick war. Unfortunately, this is a long process and with an opponent as determined as the Taliban, it could be forty years to actually get things properly functioning.

Then he started to tell me that the ministry of power cannot even provide power to the city of Kabul. Almost everyone in the city is living without power. If they have a generator, they are lucky if it powers six lights in their homes. My general, who makes decent money for Afghans, said he doesn't always have power. The people that will always have power are those "corrupt officials" running the ministries. They don't have power companies here! That floored me. I can't imagine having to depend on the government for power. Then the American side of me kicked in and thought, *No one has stepped up to be the sole power company?*

Do they know how much money they would make if they could just guarantee power for these people? I can't believe a company from India hasn't come in and taken advantage of this opportunity. While I thought that, I was still crushed that this country doesn't have the means to have a power company. It is so sad what these people deal with. I'm sickened by the fact that these people would rather cover their own butts than take care of their people. If we can't get that thought process changed, this country will not be able to survive on its own.

The first thing a good leader will teach you about being a leader is to *take care of your people*! How hard is that to comprehend? Ugh, so frustrating.

Well, I really just wanted to let you know the question my general asked me. I wish I were a superhero so I could just make it all better! Ha! I feel so helpless, and that is not good when I'm in this country doing a "job." Again I just wanted to share. Feel free to respond if you want.

Have a great day. May God bless you and keep you safe always.

Gabe was getting ready to go on his R&R to Qatar. Shortly after, I would be heading home. We talked about how we would deal with that and when we'd see each other again. I e-mailed my father about how nervous I was when Gabe and I would be separated.

From: Tiffany
Date: Tue, 6 Jan 2009
To: Donald
Subject: Fear

Daddy,

You are the only one who will understand me right now! I keep crying about Gabe. It's the same as my fear of losing you. I'm so afraid of losing the things that make me happy. I haven't had any dreams yet, but I'm sure I will soon enough, just like I have with you. I've been praying to God and trying to figure out why I have this fear, but nothing seems to come to mind. I love him so much, and I can't/don't want to imagine my life without him.

I know I need to get a hold of myself, but I don't know how. I keep trying to give Gabe to God, but I feel like as soon as I'm done praying that I take him right back. Like I have to have control even though I know the *only one* who can keep him safe is *God*. I trust that God has him in his hand and is keeping him safe, but this fear will not subside.

I'm so afraid that when he leaves Saturday it will be the last time I see him, and I just don't know if I will be able to function if that does happen. I know I can take care of myself, and I know how to be independent, but I don't want to anymore. I want to share my life with Gabe until I die.

Daddy, I've never felt like this about someone before, and I feel so lost. I love him more than I've ever loved anyone, and I think that is part of what scares me. I'm completely vulnerable to someone else for the first time ever.

I didn't want to write you to depress you or anything, but I needed to get this off my chest to someone I know would understand. I've been crying for more than thirty minutes now and just don't know if I'm gonna get to sleep if it continues. I love you bunches and miss you more. God bless you and keep you safe always.

He lovingly responded in an e-mail to encourage me.

From: Don
Date: January 6, 2009
To: Tiff
Subject: Re: Fear

Baby girl,

I wish that I could give you a big hug and make everything all right. The thing that I keep thinking is that God led you to Gabe. Then through Gabe you grew close to God again. I believe that God put you two together to live a wonderful life through him. This separation may be a test of your faith and your love for each other. I know there are no words to make the pain any less. If you can pour all yourself into your work and your studies, that won't make it any easier, but it might make time pass faster. You and Gabe lean on each other for

strength. I love you bunches, and I will be here for you. God bless and keep you safe always.
Love, Daddy

My father was right about me trusting in God. God was about to allow things to happen that would bring Gabe and I together. Gabe was working out at Bagram Air Field (BAF) when he dislocated his shoulder. That was the fourth time on the same side. The doctor told him he needed to go home for surgery or it would continue to happen.

Gabe's one-year deployment was shortened to seven months. Again I saw God orchestrate things to his will. Gabe flew home with me from Afghanistan! I was the happiest girl in the world. I sympathized with his pain but was ecstatic that he would be out of danger. Also, I could see him more often. Gabe was stationed in Arizona, and I was in Idaho, but at least we were in the same country.

Gabe and I discussed getting married at some point but hadn't yet decided when. During a phone call with my dad, he suggested, "Why don't you get married in Vegas?"

"Vegas," I repeated. Images of slot machines, endless buffets, and Elvis impersonators filled my mind. I chewed on the idea to see if I liked the texture and flavor.

"In fact, I'll pay for it," my father said; then he chuckled.

Dad and me 2009

Gabe's parents agreed. I wasn't close enough to my mother to even consider letting her know about the event. Since my father and Gabe's parents supported us, while talking on the phone, we decided to get married. Then he planned everything in only two days!

"Don't worry about an engagement ring," I mentioned before we hung up. I couldn't believe it. I was going to be Gabe's wife in only a few more sunrises. Part of me worried. *What if this marriage fails? What if I'm not good enough for him? What if I screw this up like everything else?* I took a deep breath. *This marriage will work!* My resolve set like drying concrete.

"Sure, sure, babe," he said quickly. He rarely used my real name. Instead I was some form of the word *baby, honey,* or even *punky butt.*

119

"I just want us to have bands. We can worry about the rest later."

"That sounds nice." He agreed, but Gabe had a sneaky surprise I didn't know about. When I landed in Arizona, I had my wedding dress with me and just wanted to get off the plane.

"Passengers, please remain seated," I heard announced when we landed. Then I saw Gabe walk onto the plane.

"Oh, God. No!" After the words escaped my lips, I covered my heart with my hand. It's not that I didn't want him to see me before the wedding or that I started to have doubts. I didn't like to be the center of attention. I got very uncomfortable and embarrassed easily. All of the other passengers were staring right at me. My face felt like it'd lit up in flames.

He came to my seat, knelt down on one knee, and then spoke. "We have to get engaged before getting married." He looked up at me nervously, like I might reject him. Gabe presented me with a gorgeous one-carat, emerald-cut diamond on a platinum band.

I'd told him many times while we were deployed that I would marry him tomorrow if we could. He shouldn't have had any worries about my answer.

"Tiffany Castleberry, will you marry me?"

I heard a few feminine voices deeply inhale.

it's not that serious

> Therefore a man shall leave his father and his mother and shall become united and cleave to his wife, and they shall become one flesh.
>
> Genesis 2:24 (AMP)

"Yes!"

The word came out rushed. I couldn't wait to be his wife. We were together five months by this point. He was perfect for me. I was so grateful that God changed my heart and mind to make this happen. He tore down many walls for me to feel safe enough to allow Gabe to get close to me. It was the first time I had ever allowed myself to be completely vulnerable.

We got married at the Venetian Hotel in Las Vegas, Nevada, on February 22, 2009. The guest list was very small. It included his parents; my best friend, Gini; another close girlfriend; and her husband. Gabe's cousin happened to be in town that weekend and also showed up with two friends. My dad didn't like to travel. With owning two dogs, he always had them as an excuse, so he didn't make it to the wedding.

The minister, Gabe, his mother, and I sat on a gondola in the water of our hotel. We even had to wear seat belts during the ceremony. Our loved ones watched from the platform nearby. Afterward we all ate at the hotel restaurant. The evening was filled with flashing lights from cameras, laughter, and countless kisses between my new husband and myself. My cheeks hurt from smiling and laughing all day. I was the luckiest girl in the world!

We didn't exactly get a honeymoon. The following couple days were spent first driving back to Arizona where Gabe lived. I stayed with him until I had to go back to Idaho.

In April I took two weeks leave to take care of Gabe in his home state after his surgery. For two weeks, I got to bathe, dress, and cook for him. I loved feeling needed and taking care of the one I loved. In June, we both moved to Wyoming to live and work at the same base.

We started looking at homes being built near his parents' retirement home in Buckeye, Arizona. The prices were so good we decided to build and design our own retirement home close to his parents. We went to the Air Force Academy for the AF versus army game. I spent more time watching him than the players on the field. I loved seeing him happy, especially since his friends were with us. More than anything I cherished when we were at church. He often placed his hand on the small of my back or held my hand. I knew in those moments he was proud to have me as his wife.

Before I could blink, the first half of our newlywed year was over. In August, my husband, the love of my life, started making hurtful comments.

"You're stomach is looking a little pudgy, babe," he told me one weekend. My hands touched my abdomen.

I looked down at it then back up at him with one eyebrow raised in confusion.

"You should work out," he added.

My jaw dropped, and I was devastated. "Pudgy," I repeated to myself. I was five two and usually weighed under 110 pounds. I'd never been heavy or fat because I have an overactive thyroid. That wasn't the last critical comment he made. Eventually I got to the point where I felt unattractive.

"Give me a minute," I said when he came into the bedroom while I was dressing for work a few weeks after the first instance. I didn't want him to see me naked anymore because I became so self-conscious.

I remembered John, my high school boyfriend who told me I was ugly and that no one would ever want me. Then there were other hateful words I'd heard by an assortment of people that were tattooed to my emotions. Now the word *pudgy* was added to them.

That one hurt the most. Not because of what it meant. Instead the pain came from who said it. *What if I really am worthless? Is Gabe just now figuring it out and regretting marrying me?*

The worst part about the situation was the comments about my beauty I heard from a coworker during the same time. For three months, Marshall was constantly pursuing me. His tan, muscular body was covered in tattoos. He was a bad boy, completely opposite of my husband.

My past abuse was running rampant in my head after my husband started making his critical remarks about my body. I asked Gabe to pray with me more. I wanted him to be our spiritual leader and head of our house. I requested many times for him to take the initiative and have us pray together before bed. My requests fell on deaf ears.

"We need to go to counseling," I told him once I was fully dressed. He still had on his light gray AF Academy sweats he wore to bed. I'd told him my request countless times. I needed him to understand the extent of damage my abusive past had on me. It wasn't only something that was over and done with. The fears and insecurities peered around the corner more often lately. I also wanted him to understand me before it became a major problem.

My goal was for him to learn and understand the effects of my abuse. I wanted this to come from a professional, not just me telling him. Gabe grew up in a perfect world and never experienced anything like what I did. I didn't know what else to do.

"It's not that serious," was his typical reply.

I felt stuck. How could I get him to comprehend how important this was. I felt like we were floating on blow-up rafts in a pool full of sharks. Every time I saw a fin, he'd say it was just a dolphin.

"If you won't go to therapy, at least spend some more time with me outside of work." In November, I asked my husband to come home early many times. He always had reasons that he had to stay late. I knew part of the problem was not wanting to disappoint his supervisors if he didn't excel.

We rarely went on dates. Sometimes I felt like we were little less than roommates. I just needed my husband to continue to love me and pursue me the way he did when we were dating. Even when I was hurt I still felt blessed to have him. Other than my father, I loved him more than any man I had ever known. *Maybe I'm asking too much from him*, I wondered. But every time I thought about holding my tongue before mentioning therapy, I continued on about it anyway. I felt sure that it was necessary.

His comments about my body were wearing on me. It was like a seesaw. The lower I felt with Gabe, the higher I rose with Marshall. My coworker continued to tell me how beautiful and sexy I was. I enjoyed his compliments more than I should have, and I didn't tell my husband about it.

The situation got out of hand before I knew it. I've heard about people watching a tornado approach. Sometimes they stare at it, thinking they are a safe distance away. The chances of it hitting them are slim. Suddenly it's upon them, and there's no time to get in their underground shelter. I didn't realize the damage this tornado would do to my life until it was too late.

Marshall told me some stories about his life back home and some of the things he did. I would parallel his experiences to what I'd heard a mobster's would be. It scared me. I thought, *This isn't the kind of person I can say no to.* I couldn't say no to anyone anymore after being abused sexually and physically. Because of all the circumstances, there was no way I would've done anything to upset this mob-like guy.

I knew if he ever got me alone I would be in trouble. He could physically force me to do something or hurt me. I should've told my husband the first time Marshall approached me, but I didn't know how to do that. I was so afraid of Gabe finding any reason to divorce me. *What if he was angry with me for Marshall liking me in the first place?* I didn't understand the proper way an adult would handle this situation. In times like this, Satan wasn't far away. He knew my weaknesses and knew how to exploit them.

During Marshall's and my conversation one afternoon, he told me, "I've even played Russian roulette with my father." His eyes bore into mine. I worked hard to keep my breathing steady. "I'm already scouting out areas in town to dump my next victim's body."

I watched as my mind played a potential future. Marshall stood by a pier while my husband's motionless figure quickly sunk to the bottom of the river. I knew that my Gabe's life would be in danger if I said no to my coworker's advances. I couldn't care less about my own well-being. I would have done anything to keep my husband safe.

A real event in my past replaced the last one. I remembered my mother and I wrestling on the living room floor, my father off to the side. It was the time when I started picking on her so she'd leave him alone. I loved Gabe just like I loved Daddy. I would let my body be used again. It was the only way I knew how to fight.

I prayed constantly for God's help and strength. I felt the slippery slope under my feet. Sabotage was coming. I begged God to save me from myself, but Satan knew all too well how to control me.

we need to talk

When you follow the desires of your sinful nature, the results are very clear: sexual immorality, impurity, lustful pleasures.

Galatians 5:19 (NLT)

I went against everything I knew and cheated on my husband. I never wanted it to happen. However, I let his compliments and my fears take me down the road that led to adultery. It is something I will regret for the rest of my life.

Every time left me feeling like I was not only covered with dirt but also filled internally with it. That's how I felt each time I was sexually assaulted. That didn't matter, though. I reminded myself I had to do this so my husband and I would be safe.

I was told in counseling once that a psychologist knew how old her patients were when they were in the Holocaust camps by how they reacted to situations. Traumatic experiences like that stunts your growth in a way. So I pretty much react to those situations like an eight-year-old because the molestation was the first truly traumatic experience for me. These are the reasons I wanted my husband and I to go to counseling together.

In December 2009, my husband found a photo I sent to the other guy. Of course he flipped out on me.

He was yelling, "Tiffany, *why* did you send some guy a photo?" I knew he was angry. He rarely called me by my first name.

I froze and went into defensive mode. I literally acted and reacted like a child! I feared that he would hit me, just because that's what happened with guys in the past. I felt like a child reverting back to survival mode. Of course that made my husband feel like I was hiding stuff from him. He left the house that night. I called my best friend crying and panicking.

I didn't want to lose him, but I didn't know how to respond or act properly. I had no idea what I was supposed to do to fix it. I shut down because that's what I always did in the past. I couldn't deal with confrontation. Instead I ran from it. Of course I denied everything and didn't tell Gabe what was going on or how it got to that point.

E-mail sent December 14, 2009

Hello my trusted family and friends,

I just wanted to ask you all to keep Gabe and I in your prayers. We are having some trouble right now, and we need all the family and friends we can gather to pray for us. I know the first few years are supposed to be difficult, but I think our military jobs add more stress than we need. Again, please keep us in your prayers.

Thanks and I love you, Tiffany

One person who responded out of concern was Nicole. As I read her e-mail, I pictured her five-two, petite but muscular body sitting at her computer table twirling her brown hair while reading my e-mail.

To: Tiffany
From my best friend Nicole:

What is wrong?

To Nicole:

We are fighting. We work too much and don't spend time with each other because we are exhausted at the end of the day. Guys have been hitting on me, and I enjoyed it more than I should have and probably encouraged it. He found an e-mail I sent last night that I never should have and the #&*^ hit the fan. That's the gist of it. Needless to say, we need a lot of prayers!

Tiff

To Tiff:

Oh, honey, I'm sorry. I know marriage is very hard. But just decide if this is truly what you want and need. I know you love him! Call me and we will talk. When are you going to be down here? Well, you got me if that is who you are referring to, but I'm sure you have him as well! If you don't mind me asking, what did the e-mail say?

Nicole

To Nicole:

I have no idea what it said if anything… I sent a picture to a guy that I shouldn't have. I was totally in the wrong, and I regretted it as soon as I did it, but you can't exactly take that back. We aren't exactly speaking right now—well, he isn't exactly speaking to me right now.

I don't know what I can do to make it better. I have apologized a hundred times, and I know that won't do enough. Now I am just praying he can forgive me and we can work through this. I screwed up really bad, Nicole, and I am so disappointed in myself. I don't know why I always try to sabotage the amazing things in my life.

Of course I was referring to you!

Tiff

To Tiffany:

Okay this is what I have realized about marriage. There are those great and wonderful times that seem like nothing could ever go wrong, but then there are those times where it seems that nothing can get better. During the not-so-good times, it feels good when other guys show you attention because, I'll be honest, I almost fell into the same situation.

Because if your husband is not able to show you the attention you need, then it flatters you when someone else does. And it's mysterious and scary, and it just feels good for someone to think things about you. Now I'm sure Gabe will forgive you because I'm sure he loves you as much as you love him, and if the situation were reversed, what would you want to hear to make it better?

That is always what I ask myself, and some things just take time. So give him a little space. But still make sure that he knows you're sorry and you regret it and you love him, which he already knows these things, but it's always good to remind him. But it is so hard when everyone has a busy schedule to spend quality time together.

Gabe and I drove from Cheyenne, Wyoming, to Cedar Creek Lake, Texas, to visit my daddy for Christmas. It was a difficult trip to say the least. I couldn't tell him what happened. I was so scared to lose him. Part of the reason I wanted to keep the affair from him was because he'd commented in the past that if I cheated on him he would be gone. Of course I never intended on doing that. I never wanted to hurt my husband. He was the love of my life. Gabe was the first person I was vulnerable with and gave myself to completely.

While we were in Texas, he kept asking about it. "I know there is more you are hiding."

I didn't want to tell him on Christmas day, so I kept putting it off. I confided in Dad the next day.

"Daddy, I cheated on Gabe. I don't know what to do." I stared at the floor until I finished my confession. Then I hesitantly looked up into his eyes. He gave me a look that portrayed he was shocked and disappointed. My heart sank. The thought of disappointing my daddy crushed my spirit.

"I know it was a horrible mistake. I never meant to hurt Gabe." I didn't tell him anything else.

A few years after my parents divorced, I learned that my mom cheated on my dad while they were married. I knew my father would have an opinion of how I should tell my husband.

"Don't tell him because it will hurt him worse." He took a deep breath and then exhaled slowly.

I never expected my dad to give me that advice. I thought for sure I would get a long speech about how to gently break it to him and how to beg for forgiveness. I listened to my dad on nearly everything he gave me advice on, but not this time. I truly believed in my heart that my true love and I were strong enough to make it through this.

Before we left Texas, I told my husband.

"Gabe, I cheated on you." We lay next to each other on my bed. His eyes widened, and his mouth opened partially. I looked at him and continued holding his hands.

"I'm so sorry. I never meant for it to happen." I was crying like a baby who had just been frightened. I didn't tell him why or that I felt I was keeping him safe. We cried and talked for a while. Then I said, "Are you going to leave me?" It was the hardest question I'd ever asked anyone. If there'd been an earthquake tearing the floor of the house apart at that moment, I wouldn't have noticed.

"We will work through it," he responded. The Tin Man getting his heart was nothing to the love I felt at that moment. "What are you afraid of?" he asked.

"Losing you." I was willing to do anything to repair the damage I had caused. Our drive back home was awful. He was so hurt and mad at me. I couldn't do anything to make it better.

"I won't tell my parents," he said out of the blue as his hands gripped the steering wheel tightly. I looked at him, but he kept his eyes on the road. "I know they wouldn't react well. I don't want you to deal with what my dad had to go through with my mom's parents.

We recognized we had a long, hard road ahead of us like any couple in our situation. The difference that made ours worse was related to our careers. I was leaving January 9 for combat skills training in New Jersey for a month. Then I was off to Iraq for six months. He was going to Afghanistan in February. We would not be together for over eight months. That was going to create more obstacles for us while we tried to rebuild our relationship.

Before I left, we daily sat and talked about everything for hours. I tried to help him understand how my past played a part. My husband could not understand why I would do something like that or how I allowed myself to be put in that position.

"I'm not trying to make excuses. I just need you to try to understand. I take complete responsibility for everything that happened." I didn't want him thinking I was trying to blame someone else.

I planned a romantic night for us before I had to fly out for training. We ate at the Melting Pot in Ft. Collins, Colorado. There were roses and wine. Then I booked a room at the Hilton and ordered the romance package. Strawberries and champagne were waiting for us when we arrived. I wanted him to see I was putting 110 percent into working through this. We had an amazing night. I believed our marriage stood a strong chance in lasting even though we wouldn't see each other for the next eight months.

We both cried at the airport when I left. I didn't want to let him go. While I was in New Jersey, we texted and called each other many times throughout the day. He never told me he was having a really hard time dealing with things while I was gone.

On Monday, February 8, 2010, I knew our communication was strained. Something wasn't right, but he wouldn't tell me anything during our conversation. Then Tuesday at 6:00 p.m. I called him on the hallway phone.

"We need to talk," he said. He sounded so calm. "I told my parents what happened. I want a divorce." He mentioned a couple days before our call he ended up informing his parents what I did. He relayed to me their opinion. They told him to divorce me immediately and called me many names.

My body went into convulsions. I fell to the floor while my heart pounded with pain. I started crying and screaming. My hands went numb. "No," I kept saying over and over. "Please don't make that decision yet." I felt like my soul was ripping in two.

He was in Little Rock, Arkansas, getting ready to leave for Afghanistan. I tried everything I could to leave training early to fly there. I didn't care about my career or anything at that point. All I wanted was to see him and try to save my marriage. That was all that mattered to me. My training commander wouldn't let me go.

I cried out to God for help. *Lord, please give me the strength and patience to follow your will and do all that I can to save, restore, and redeem our beautiful marriage. Father, please never leave Gabe's side. Keep him safe, and heal his heart. I love you and praise you. All this I ask in Jesus's name. Amen.*

Over the next couple of days, I couldn't eat, and I wasn't sleeping. I cried all the time and talked to my dad about what I could do. He sent my husband an e-mail trying to plead my case. It stated my father understood what Gabe was going through.

I talked to Daddy one more time on the phone. I cried and told him how much I loved my husband. I didn't know that would be the last conversation I would ever have with my daddy.

facing my two greatest fears at once

For God has made my heart faint, timid, and broken, and this Almighty has terrified me because I was not cut off before the darkness [of these woes befell me], neither has He covered the thick darkness from my face.

Job 23:16-17 (AMP)

On Friday, February 12, 2010, I couldn't get Daddy on the phone. I sent a couple of e-mails first thing that morning because Texas had received a record snowfall. I was curious what Daddy would say about it or how the girls (dogs) reacted to it.

That day I was with my friend Jodi, my roommate during CST. Her big smile and positive attitude was about to be needed. Her mom, who had a similar shade of strawberry blond hair and green eyes, and aunt were also with us. We had been touring around Princeton and looking at different bookstores throughout the day. When we were at Barnes and Noble, I couldn't stand it anymore. Even though we'd talked the day before, I felt like something was wrong and just could not shake that feeling. I hadn't received an e-mail back from Dad, and that was hours ago. I tried to call a few times while

I was walking around the store. We sat down for coffee, and my heart just wouldn't stop racing. I tried to pray and ask for God's peace, but it just wasn't working.

We left the store, and I called Susan, my godmother who had the same salt-and-pepper hair as my father. She had a huge heart and often filled in for my mom as a good role model. She wasn't answering the phone either. I panicked and felt my heart ache as it skipped a beat. I tried a couple more times, but no answer. I called my best friend, Nicole, and tried to explain the situation as best I could without freaking out.

Finally, I just said, "I need you to go to the house and check on Daddy." She said she would do that and then she would call me when she got there.

It felt like an eternity while I was waiting to hear back from Nicole. I stared at my phone as if that would make it ring. Susan called back while I was waiting for Nicole. I told her what was going on and asked her to go over to the house as well. She let me go and headed over to Dad's house.

Shortly after I hung up with Susan, although it felt like an eternity, Nicole called. Before she could say anything, I swear my heart stopped.

"Tiff, I'm knocking on the door, and I can see him on the couch, but he isn't getting up. The dogs are going crazy."

I don't remember anything after that. I know they called the cops, and Susan and Nicole were there together when they arrived. The police had to break down the front door because everything was locked.

At this point, I was in a vehicle. "I need out of the car!"

Jodi pulled into the next gas station. I stepped outside then walked about ten feet and fell down. I kept saying, "God, this cannot be happening," over and over. It was difficult to breathe through my tears. At that moment, my world collapsed on top of me.

I called Gabe and said, "Daddy is gone."

"What?" he asked, confused.

"Daddy is dead. I need you to call someone so you don't have to go to Afghanistan right away. I need you with me."

"I will."

I don't remember the journey from the gas station to the base. Once we arrived, I realized where I was. I walked in the building and collapsed in the day room. I couldn't see because I was crying so hard. I could barely breathe.

I heard someone ask if I was okay. I had three people around me. One of them said, "She just found out her father passed away."

Lieutenant Colonel Biggs started calling people for me. He figured out how to get the official notification of my father's death routed properly. That way I could take emergency leave and have my Iraq deployment canceled. I phoned family and friends immediately to let them know.

I tried so hard to be strong during the conversations, but I broke down constantly. I shook and felt numb each time I had to say that dreaded sentence: "Daddy passed away."

Hearing his sisters burst into tears on the other end of the phone ripped me apart even more. My daddy was the middle of seven kids—five girls and two boys. He was the first one to die. He was healthy, so no one ever expected it…least of all me.

I struggled between each phone call and could barely breathe. I had to telephone my commander. "With the impending divorce and my dad passing away, I will not be able to deploy to Iraq this time."

"I understand," she replied.

"Can you talk to my husband's Commander about getting him back for my dad's funeral?" I knew I'd need him to support me.

"I'll do what I can."

The earliest flight I could get out of New Jersey was Saturday morning. My coworkers kept trying to get me to consume food. I hadn't had more than three or four bites of anything since my husband said he wanted a divorce. After finding out about my dad, eating was nearly impossible.

The people that drove me to the airport attempted to get me to talk, but I just sat and stared out of the back-seat window. I kept telling myself, *There is no way this can be happening. There is no way I would have to face my two greatest fears at one time! How am I going to survive losing my husband, my world, and my father, my lifeline? How could God possibly believe I am strong enough to live to tell this tale?*

During the flight, I thought about my past. I was so grateful my father and I never left anything unsaid. He told me many times before his sudden passing from a heart attack that he was proud of me and that I was his hero. I didn't know how I could be his hero, but I knew everything I did was to make him proud.

He told me once that when I was born he thought he would never have to worry about me going to war or being in harm's way since I was a girl. He sure was wrong about that! I deployed for three different wars/conflicts, and that's where I preferred to be. I have always been a tomboy, and I would never call myself girly. I would rather wrestle a boy than go shopping for shoes. I loved him more than I could ever describe and knew I would miss him terribly every day.

I arrived at the Dallas/Ft. Worth airport. As much as I wanted to see my godmother, Susan, and best friend, Nicole, I also dreaded it. I knew when my eyes met theirs, I would uncontrollably burst into tears. That is exactly what happened. I wished I could curl up in a ball on the floor and sob it all away.

I had to relive the truth of my father's death every time I encountered someone for the first time. Seeing loved ones reminded me that my daddy was really gone. This wasn't just some unbearable, repetitive nightmare.

Nicole brought Jaci, her five-month-old baby girl, to the airport. At that moment, a new revelation hit me. *If I ever have children, they will not get to meet their amazing grandfather, "Pop."* I started crying again as I realized my entire life had been changed, and there was nothing I could do about it. I was slowly recognizing the depth of what it meant not to have my daddy with me anymore. This eye-opener was only the beginning of things to come.

We drove from Dallas to Gun Barrel City, talking about anything except the reason I was home. That hour-and-a-half ride was different than any other. I stared out the window. The world hadn't changed, but I felt like everything should have stopped the moment my daddy was gone.

The closer we got to his house, the more my insides twisted and wrenched. My father's place had always been my safe haven. I loved being there because it always made me feel relaxed and calm. This time it was eerie, quiet, and missing the main ingredient: my daddy. I wanted more than anything to see him, hold him tight, and never let him go. I wanted to tell him a million times that I loved him, knowing it would never be enough and couldn't cover the depth of my true feelings.

I got a phone call from my husband as we turned onto Dad's street.

"Don't worry about us. We will be fine. You need to focus on your father."

"Thanks, Gabe. I miss you."

"Me too. I'll do what I can to get to Texas to be with you."

The next morning I read an e-mail from him. It was horribly cold. He stated he wasn't coming back and that there was nothing I could do to change that. He wrote I needed to realize our marriage was over and accept that. As I got to the end, I wondered, *Who does that to someone they love when they just lost a parent who meant the world to them?*

I thought about Colossians 3:12-13 (NLT):

> Since God chose you to be the holy people he loves, you must clothe yourselves with tender-hearted mercy, kindness, humility, gentleness, and patience. Make allowance for each other's

faults, and forgive anyone who offends you. Remember, the Lord forgave you, so you must forgive others.

I figured it was his parents pushing him to act like that. It ripped my heart into a million pieces. I had never been so shattered, broken, and abandoned like I was at that time. My friends wanted to be there for me, but the only person *I* wanted by my side was my husband!

His parents had been so supportive and loving when I first met them and while Gabe and I were together. They were such sweet and approachable Christians.

"You're not our daughter-in-law. You are our daughter," they'd said. His mother and father always prayed for me and spoke of God's love, grace, and mercy. I felt like I was an accepted part of the family. Once my husband told them what I did, they cut me off and never spoke to me again.

What happened to their Christian attitudes? I thought about Matthew 18:21-22 (NLT):

> Then Peter came to him and asked, "Lord, how often should I forgive someone who sins against me? Seven times?"
>
> "No, not seven times," Jesus replied, "But seventy times seven!"

Christ told us to forgive seventy times seven times and to turn the other cheek. I was discarded by them. *How could they call themselves Christians and yet be so cold to anyone during such a traumatic time?*

Once I'd learned his parents were aware of our marital problems, I went beyond trying to repair things with just my husband. I sent his parents multiple e-mails apologizing and trying to explain the situation. I continued to seek their forgiveness all while still dealing with my father's unexpected death.

I prayed and searched Scripture constantly, trying to figure out what to do and how to pray. I sent my husband's mom multiple e-mails asking for forgiveness and expressing my humble remorse. I sent Mother's Day e-mails telling her I was blessed to have her in my life and I thanked God for her always. I sent more messages on holidays and birthdays and never received any response. I was dead to his family. There was no unconditional love, grace, mercy, or forgiveness coming from them anymore.

I asked for their pardon and swore never to do anything like that again. I professed my love for their son and spilled my guts. I never got a response from them at all. They didn't care that I was trying to make things better or that I took responsibility for everything.

My insides were ripped to shreds. I felt like I was going through the process for grounding meat, but I looked fine on the outside. I have a picture of my English Mastiff in my lap while I'm sitting on the floor at my dad's house. I look like I'm comatose. My godmother, aunts, and friends were packing up the house and moving stuff around me.

I barely remember anything about being at home for those ten days. My dad would've been so proud of his sisters for their support. My aunt Peggy and aunt Sandi were there for me from the moment I called them with the horrible news and even still are now.

I went to the funeral home to settle arrangements for my dad's cremation and service. There was an entourage with me wherever I traveled. Everyone wanted to be there for me and help in any way they could. I think secretly they all were quietly waiting for me to internally combust.

As I spoke to the funeral director, I remembered my daddy and I arguing about whether or not he should be cremated. He *did not* want to be buried in a box for the worms to eat. In addition to that, he always wanted to make sure I knew where his important documents were.

Every time he said, "When I'm gone…" I would jump in and say, "You are not going to die." Or I'd reply, "No, I don't want to talk about this." I did listen though. I knew exactly where all of his necessary paperwork was and that he wanted to be cremated. As much as the thought of my dad being burned killed me, I did what he asked for.

For some reason, it took a while to acquire his body back from the Dallas medical examiner. I reminded myself a thousand times it was just a body. It wasn't actually him burning, and he wasn't in pain. When we finally got him, I asked the funeral home to prepare my father so I could see him. I knew that it would never be real in my mind if I couldn't look at him one last time.

When I did see him, I thought, *That's not my daddy.* It didn't look like him because his stomach was partially caved in, and his face looked fat. I thank God that image doesn't haunt me like it does for a lot of people. I can hardly remember it. Many loved ones didn't think I should see him that way, but I needed it. I had to look at him lying there to believe he wasn't coming back.

There were some funny times during those ten days. One of them involved my crazy aunts Peggy and Sandi drugging me every night to make sure I slept. I had no idea what they were giving me, but it helped.

They tried to force food down my throat too. When food didn't work, they got me alcohol. I guess that made sense at the time. Those two tried to fatten me up my entire life and are still trying to today!

My best friends Gini and Trey were with me during that time as well. It was bittersweet. I loved having everyone around, but I hated why they were all there.

One of my closest friends from high school who my dad loved was Kevin Ray Passons. He was there every step of the way as well. Kevin was a senior when I was a freshman in high school. For some insane reason, my dad thought Kevin was trustworthy enough to take care of me even at our young ages.

Kevin and I grew up and got smarter, but in high school we were always finding trouble. Daddy told Kevin, "You better take care of my baby girl or I'm gonna come after you." Kevin always brought me home safe, but we both understood God watched over us.

I knew I wouldn't be able to speak one sentence at my dad's funeral. Even if I could've, the words wouldn't have been understandable to those in the audience. Therefore, I asked Kevin if he would speak at Daddy's service since they had a special relationship. I knew that would've made my father proud. Kevin said he would be honored to get up and speak.

He did such an awesome job. Kevin surpassed every expectation I had. I know Daddy was so grateful for his kind words and his outside view of our relationship. I cried so hard and loud through the entire service.

I couldn't find Dad's DD214 to prove he was in the air force, so I wasn't able to get an honor guard for his service. Since Trey and Gini were in the army and knew how much it meant to me, they bought a flag, folded it, and presented it to me at the end of the service. I had no idea they were going to do that for me. It was a small gesture, but having a flag at his funeral since he served honorably in Vietnam mattered.

Dad's AF picture

Those veterans were spit on, called baby killers, and disrespected when they returned home. The least I could do was have a flag folded in his honor. I know people came up to me after the service to pay their respects and love on me, but I don't really remember that part.

Throughout the ten days I was at home preparing things for Dad's funeral and getting his house cleared out, I received e-mails from my husband. He went back and forth about us. Some were sympathetic about what was going on. Then the next were cold as frostbite, telling me we were only going to communicate about the divorce through lawyers.

The only thing I can compare it to is the highs and lows of someone with bipolar disorder. I went through highs, thinking our marriage might make it, to lows after Gabe stated otherwise.

I was constantly fighting for our marriage, apologizing for everything and asking what I could do to make it up to him. Dealing with these traumatic events simultaneously was probably a major rationale for my aunts drugging me. One moment I was crying about my dad, and in the next second I was howling about my husband.

The one person I wanted by my side more than anyone was the same individual making this tragic time more excruciating. I prayed to God to take me home every night and again every morning when I woke up. I had nothing inside of me that wanted to live another moment. In those days at my father's home, I begged God to take my life countless times.

I became a Christian when I was in high school. I just happened to make friends with the right crowd. I have never been perfect, and I am a sinner every moment of my life. My faith was the only reason I didn't take my life after my dad's funeral. I didn't care what the rest of my family and friends would think or if they would miss me.

The two most important people in my life were gone, and I did not want to live one day without them. I felt like I was being fed through a wood chipper. Sometimes sleep was the only way to get away from it. Eventually I started having nightmares and woke up crying while my body convulsed.

My dad had my English Mastiff. Because I was deploying so much, I couldn't keep her. He also had a Great Pyrenees, Jezzebell, which was always by his side. She had just turned nine in December while my husband and I were home for Christmas. Dad and I had discussed putting her to sleep because she had horrible arthritis in her hips, and her eyes had stopped making tears. He said, "I just couldn't do it because it would be like cutting off my right arm." So we let her live.

Unfortunately, now that Dad was gone, I knew Jezzy would not last long without him. I had to decide if I wanted to bring her and my Mastiff back to Wyoming or let Jezzy go. I asked my godmother to call the vet so we could put her down.

We took the dog to the vet, and I laid her 130-pound body in my lap. I wanted to hold her until she was gone.

"I love you. You'll be with Pop shortly," I whispered in her right ear. I cried like a baby and held her long after she was gone. I knew she wasn't in any more pain and that she was by my daddy's side again. However, it was so hard to let her go.

Shortly after the second death I had to deal with that month, I said good-bye to everyone, including my aunts. They continued to check on me often after we parted ways. I imagined Daddy grinning as he looked down from heaven at their kindness. I'm especially grateful to those women because we weren't always close.

God would never leave me in my darkest hour

I have strength for all things in Christ Who empowers me [I am ready for anything and equal to anything through Him Who infuses inner strength into me; I am self-sufficient in Christ's sufficiency].

Philippians 4:13 (AMP)

Even though I was not ready to go back to work, I didn't have any more leave. I had a very long twenty-two-hour drive back to Wyoming alone in Dad's SUV. I wasn't using any more drugs to sleep through everything. Instead I was faced with a harsh reality of my upside-down world. My drive consisted of thousands of tears, yelling, and many prayers to God. I was shouting at my dad for leaving me and telling him I needed him more than ever. I said, "If I find out this could have been prevented by you just going to the doctor, I'm going to strangle you."

I replayed the last time we talked over and over. I tried to remember if I'd asked if he was feeling okay. Our conversation only ended because we got cut off.

He called back and left a voice-mail. I wished that he hadn't left me during this time in my life while I was so upset and broken.

I asked myself, Was there anything I could have done differently to keep him around longer? It's amazing I didn't wreck because I drove while I was crying rivers and could barely see. My sweet English Mastiff must have thought I'd lost my mind. She could tell I was upset because she kept trying to put her head on my shoulder from the back seat. Little did my baby girl know she was the second reason I needed to make it through this.

As I got closer to our house in Wyoming, thoughts poured into my head. I dreaded sleeping in Gabe's and my bed alone. The thought of even walking into our first home together knowing everything was in shambles made me sick to my stomach. Our pictures were all over the house, and his smell haunted me when I walked in. After getting Missy, my Mastiff, settled in, I laid on our bed, curled into a ball, and cried. It didn't help that it was our wedding anniversary, February 22, 2010. I sent my husband an e-mail telling him how much I loved him and wanted God to help us get through this.

Missy

During this time, I still wasn't in a good relationship with my mother. Since my parents got divorced, my relationship with her had been extremely dysfunctional. I dodged most of her phone calls. It got to a point where every one of them was a guilt trip or her crying about something. I didn't have the patience or compassion to deal with it.

My mom knew I got money from Dad's life insurance and selling the house.

"You need to give me $15,000," she boldly stated over the phone during a short conversation.

That infuriated me. I didn't want to talk to her after that call. Besides dealing with my mom, most of February was a teary blur. I went back to work, and my commander told me to take it easy and go home when I became overwhelmed. In the beginning, I did a few half days, but it got to the point when I felt like it would help more to keep myself busy. So I was working full days in no time. When at home, I was a sobbing mess. I would curl up next to Missy and cry for long periods. It was helpful that she liked to sleep eighteen hours a day or she never would have laid there while I did that.

My cuddly Missy

At the end of February, I broke down over something simple and meaningless in the grand scheme of things. My dad always renewed my vehicle registration in Texas. Therefore, it wasn't something I thought about. I happened to glance at my registration sticker on my windshield on February 27, 2010 and noticed my tags expired March 1, 2010!

I burst into tears for two reasons. The first one was my dad was gone and this was just another reminder. The second one was I had to give up my Texas plates and register my vehicle in Wyoming. I remember driving down the highway looking up at heaven and yelling at my dad about my truck registration. I'm sure he was laughing at me, but I was very upset about giving up my Texas plates.

My daddy's birthday was coming too quickly for me. I was dreading March 8. Oddly, the night before, the shrill of my phone ringing woke me up around ten o'clock. It was my husband on the other end of the line.

"I missed my wife," he said. "Can we talk?"

"Sure," I said, relieved to hear his voice.

"Go into the guest room and look on the floor in the closet."

Drowsy and still half asleep, I went into the other room. Under his green laundry bag was a 2010 calendar he created with pictures of us. I opened it, and the first photo I saw was my husband, me, and Daddy sitting on the couch at Dad's house. I burst into tears.

"That wasn't the response I expected," he replied after hearing my sobs.

I explained to him the first picture I saw so he would understand my reaction. The calendar was beautiful, with some of the sweetest captions that went along with the photos. Under one of my pictures, he wrote, "Perfect for me." That was one of our little sayings because we knew no one was perfect, but we always said we were perfect for each other.

I went back to lie in bed as we talked on the phone. I asked him, "What does this mean? Are we working on us?"

"Yes, I guess it does," he said.

"I need you to answer one question for me. Why didn't you come home for Dad's funeral?"

"I don't know," was all he said.

A few days later we talked on the phone again. This time he had an answer to my question. He told me, "I didn't come back because I didn't want to talk about or work on us."

I never said it out loud, but I thought, *Are you kidding me? Get over yourself. It was about my daddy and paying respect to him and your relationship.* It killed me he looked at it like that. My dad always loved and treated Gabe like he was his own son. If anyone else in my life had done that to me when my dad passed away, I would have cut them out of my life and never thought twice about it. I know that's not a good thing to say or anything to be proud of, but that was how I always dealt with stuff like that. However, I wasn't going to do that with my husband. For the first time, I truly loved someone unconditionally. I prayed daily that I would never resent my husband for abandoning me at my greatest time of need. I needed to forgive him and love him as Christ loves us.

Every day I did my best to show Gabe I loved him and was truly dedicated to making this horrible betrayal up to him. I felt handicapped, though, since he was in Afghanistan while I was in Wyoming. I tried to call or e-mail him daily. I took any chance I had to keep him from worrying I'd repeat my mistake. Any time I passed a male in the hallway, I would go straight to my office and e-mail my husband about it. I'd let Gabe know exactly what was said. I prayed for God to heal our hearts and help us trust each other more and more every day.

I was still crying a lot about missing my daddy, but I was so focused on saving and restoring my marriage, I had almost put the mourning process on the back burner. I read a ton of books on saving a marriage. They focused on the fact that love is a choice, how to win my husband back, and love languages. I sent pictures and told him not only how much I missed him but also the tremendous amount he meant to me. I wanted to grow old with him. He responded, letting me know he missed me and I was his one and only, no matter what. We discussed that we both meant our vows and wanted to work through things. During some of our conversations, there was discussion about taking a needed vacation when he returned from Afghanistan so we could get away from everyone else and focus on us.

About mid-March, I woke up in the middle of the night because my heart was hurting. It was nothing like chest pains but instead similar to how a bruise felt when it was hit. Except this was constant for a few minutes until it finally vanished like everything was fine. I started praying constantly, asking God to speak to my husband's heart, help him open up to me, and discuss his concerns. I felt like someone else had Gabe's ear. Part of the reason was he wouldn't really dive deep into our issues. When I asked his thoughts, he would just change the subject. I knew he was hurting and questioning things, but since he wouldn't talk to me about it, I couldn't do anything.

During one of our phone conversations, he told me, "My parents are having a very hard time with us working on our marriage. They have no desire to see you again and aren't sure they ever would."

"I will pray for them, but they need to trust God and you right now." I tried to keep my tone positive. While I was annoyed at Gabe's parents, I didn't want him thinking I was trying to place a wedge between him and them. "I had no intention of making things difficult between you and your parents. My main concern is us working through things and becoming stronger." My eyes were beginning to pool with tears.

"No matter what, you are my one and only. We will be okay." His words were like soothing aloe to a tomato-red sunburn.

A week later Gabe let me know his mom was sending him a letter. He didn't say anything else or imply what it was about. At that moment, I felt my heart start hurting again. Something worried me immensely, and I had no idea what it was or why. He continued to tell me how much he loved me and couldn't wait to get home. We even discussed kids' names and growing old together. I just kept praying God would continue to work in us and make us stronger so we could glorify his name.

Although things seemed to be working out in my marriage, it felt like every time I turned around something else was being thrown at me. I was having some medical issues checked, but I wasn't really concerned. Then I got the call telling me I could have breast cancer and would need to have another ultrasound in six months. They found a cyst on my liver and currently weren't sure about it. That wasn't all. I was also told at my hospital appointment that day I might have bladder cancer and would need to be screened over the next month. I literally walked out of the building, looked up at the sky, and said out loud, "Really?" My next thought was, *Okay, Satan, bring it on!*

The next day I told my husband all the possibilities the doctors said. He encouraged me and seemed so supportive and loving. Although he was in another country, it was as if he was by my side.

I felt in my soul God telling me that when, not if, Gabe and I worked through all of the hard stuff, we would be so much stronger on the other side and blessed beyond belief. I believed that promise at the core of my soul and trusted God wholly. I clung to that promise when fear would rise up. My husband had already gone back and forth a number of times about us. As much as I trusted God, a small part of me was waiting for him to pull the rug out from under me again. I knew Gabe had free will, and that worried me. God made that promise to me, but he wouldn't force my husband to stay and work to restore our marriage.

Later that week, and a day before he got the letter from his mom, we were in harmony and doing well.

Gabe continued to tell me how much he missed me and loved me, as I did him. The last e-mail that day was him telling me he loved me more than anything and no matter what I was his one and only. I went to bed that night hopeful but woke up around midnight in a cold sweat. I was grasping for air, my heart was pounding, and it felt like my insides were contracting. I saw the light blinking on my phone informing me I had a new e-mail. I grabbed it and saw it was from my husband. The subject line stated, "Us." I opened it immediately to discover he wrote our relationship was over. He couldn't trust me and didn't want to work on things. My breathing became more difficult. I replied, telling him "No! Call me so we can talk about this. Don't do this through an e-mail."

I honestly thought I was going to have a heart attack right then. I could not believe he would make this decision and tell me in an e-mail. I went to the bathroom to try and catch my breath. I lay down on the cold tile because I felt like my temperature was 110, and my entire body was throbbing. I wept while every fiber of my being hurt and prayed to God for some kind of understanding.

I constantly cried out to God for help. Some days were better than others. During them, I focused on being grateful in my prayers.

> Jesus,
>
> I thank you for your unfailing love and for giving your life for my sins. I give you my life, my marriage, my work, family, and friends. Take control and execute your perfect will in my life.

I don't want to have control of anything because you are the one to lead me perfectly. I love you and praise you for all of my blessings moment by moment. In you only do I trust and lean on. All these things in Jesus's holy name. Amen.

On the days when it seemed like the heaviness of sadness would never go away, I had different prayers. I cried out to God like David did in the Psalms, begging for help and for him to take my life.

Lord God Almighty, I come to you broken this morning. My fear is rising up, and although I know you will take care of us, it is still here. I trust you, and I want you in complete control of my life. I'm just having a difficult time shaking this.

"If God is for us, who can be against us?" I want to give all of my fears to you, Lord God. I know you have a perfect will for our lives, and I trust that. Help me, Jesus, to continually give Gabe's safety to you. Please forgive me for failing you, and help me to forgive those who hurt and fail me.

Oh, Jesus, help me to strengthen my faith in you daily. Draw me close to you. I love you and praise you. In Jesus's name. Amen. Lord, restore my marriage.

On April 12, I reached my breaking point. I couldn't handle the thought of Gabe never being part of my life again. I was also still grieving the loss of my father. I sent this e-mail to my friends.

I know most of you will not want to hear this, but I won't let anyone ever say, "Well, I just didn't know…" I have hit my breaking point. I'm not stable, and I can't tell anyone anything positive right now. I'm crying all the time, and things are not getting easier. I'm praying all the time and begging God to take me home. I don't want to be here anymore, and if that makes me a bad person, oh well. I'm not perfect, and I never will be. I'm completely alone, and I am not handling any of this well anymore.

Please before any one puts me down or says something positive, put yourself in my place. I have lost my loving, wonderful father and my husband. I have medical issues, and every time I turn around, there is something new. I'm not Job, even though I keep praising God. I pray all the time, but it is a horrible thing when you are going through all of this and have *no one* to hug you or to cry on their shoulder. I'm expected to be perfect and put together at work every day, and I am just not capable of keeping this charade going much longer.

Just to give you a real idea of how I feel in case anyone is in denial, here is a song I have on repeat:

"One Foot Wrong" by Pink

Am I sweating, or are these tears on my face?
Should I be hungry? I can't remember the last time that I ate.
Call someone; I need a friend to talk me down.
But one foot wrong and I'm gonna fall.

Somebody gets it, somebody gets it,
But one foot wrong and I'm gonna fall.
Somebody gets it, somebody gets it.
All the lights are on, but I'm in the dark.
Who's gonna find me, who's gonna find me?
Just one foot wrong.
You'll have to love me when I'm gone.
Does anyone see this?
Lucky me, I guess I'm the chosen one.
Color and madness
First in line I put my money down.
Some freedom, it's the tiniest hell in town.
Some people find the beauty in all of this.
I go straight to the dark side, the abyss.
If it's bad, is it always my fault?
Oh, did somebody bring me down? Did some-
body bring me down? Did somebody bring me
down?
Have to love me when I'm gone.
Love me when I'm gone.
You'll have to love me when I'm gone. You'll
have to love me when I'm gone.

Does that sound like a person who is okay?
Two months later [after] my world turned
upside down. I'm still living this nightmare.
I'm sorry if this bothers you, but I can't tell you
how many times I've prayed and asked God to
take me home in the last four days.

I'll tell you the same thing I've been telling
God: I don't want to live one day after Gabe
leaves me. This life is not worth anything without my daddy or Gabe to share it with. I can't

163

see ever taking my own life, but I will continue to pray, "God, if he leaves, take me home the next day." I'm so tired of having to move on and being expected to be perfect in the process. I'm human… I suck, and I don't do things perfectly. Forgive me for being real, but I can't hide my shattered world.

I knew that it hurt my godmother and friends when I said I lost everything and was all alone. They took it personally. I never wanted to wound anyone's feelings, but that was honestly how I felt.

I had a revelation on the way to work one morning in late April. The night before I tried to get a hold of Gabe. I had some questions that I wanted answers to, and he was the only person who could give them to me. No one picked up his phone, so I sent him an e-mail. It asked him to call me at the end of his workday so we could discuss some things.

I received a response from him the next morning telling me I needed to realize our relationship was over. He wrote that he didn't want to discuss working on our relationship. He said we could discuss the divorce, but everything else could go through e-mail.

I responded and told him I had some questions he needed to answer so I could understand everything that was going on. I wrote that I wouldn't be emotional.

During that time, I always began my mornings with a Christian mix of music so I started each day praising

God. The right songs were shuffling around helping me be in a great mood. As I began my drive to work, the revelation hit me. I thought, *I need to focus on what kind of man would leave me in my darkest hour when he claims to love me so dearly.*

Then I started talking out loud to Jesus. "God, why would any man who claims to love someone so dearly abandon her knowing it was her darkest hour and greatest fear? Why?"

A Kirk Franklin song came on. I started singing along, praising God and raising my hands in the truck. I didn't care if people in other neighboring cars thought I was nuts. Then I started crying and realized that *God* would never leave me in my darkest hour.

He was with me through all of that pain and loved me unconditionally. I shouted above the music, "Praise God and his glorious love!" A calm feeling came over me. I knew that He would get me through this like everything else. God would provide an amazing journey. Although I'd lost two people whom I loved so very much, I would be okay.

I had the comfort of knowing that my "perfect for me" earthly father was with the one true perfect Father in heaven now. I began to understand my daddy would always be with me no matter how much I missed him.

I thought about how I was blessed to have such an awesome father who always supported me and told me he loved me. My dad was great, and I knew I would never stop cherishing the years I had with him. I replayed in my mind the many times he'd told me over the last few years, "I'm proud of you. Baby girl, you're my hero." Those things I would never lose, and I will always cherish. I praised God for such an amazing revelation that morning.

God knew how much I'd need that understanding. In spite of my new inspiration, April was a very difficult month. As much as I tried to keep busy at work, it wasn't doing anything for me. I got home and cried from the moment I walked in the door to the time I went to bed. Most of the sobbing was in the middle of the floor curled up in a ball while my body convulsed from crying so hard.

My eyes always burned. I went from being a person who hardly ever cried to a constant waterfall. When *New Moon* in the Twilight Saga came out, I watched Bella's dreams and her sitting in the chair just staring off. Her nightmares where she screamed while curled up in pain and then woke up, that was my real life for months. I had never felt that kind of pain in my body and heart. One moment I was crying about missing my husband, and the next I was crying because my daddy was gone.

Every day I still begged God to take my life. I wanted to be with him and my daddy again. There is no doubt in my mind that if I were not a Christian I would have taken my life without any second thought. My friends and family were in other states, and I was literally alone in Wyoming going through everything. There were people at work who pretended to be my friends and acted like they cared, but it was fake. They all ended up turning their backs on me.

Throughout the rest of the month and on into the next one, I constantly begged God to restore my marriage.

> Lord God Almighty,
>
> Thank you for this day and allowing me to wake up. Forgive me for failing you, and continually help me to forgive those around me. I want to focus on you Jesus like Isaiah 26:3-4 (NLT) that says, "You will keep in perfect peace all who trust in you, all whose thoughts are fixed on you. Trust in the Lord always, for the Lord God is the eternal Rock." I want to walk in your truth, Lord, as in Psalm 86:11 (AMP): "Teach me Your way, O Lord, that I may walk and live in Your truth; direct and unite my heart [solely, reverently] to fear and honor Your name."
>
> I love you and praise you, Jesus. Please comfort me in my difficult times. We are told to boldly say what we want you to do for us: I want my marriage restored! You are the only one who can do this. Please heal our hearts and take our pain away. Restore us, Lord, with a stronger relationship. Thank you for all you do in our lives. In Jesus's name I pray. Amen.

I bought the book *Love Dare* and started writing in the workbook sections daily. I asked God to open my husband's heart. Nothing seemed to matter. Then Friday, May 7, I heard a knock at the door shortly after I got home from work. Something inside told me not to answer it.

you're not alone

"But reach out and take away his health, and he will surely curse you to your face!" Satan replied.

"All right, do with him as you please," the LORD said to Satan. "But spare his life."

Job 2:5-6 (NLT)

I opened the door and was served with divorce papers. I closed the door and fell to the floor, screaming and crying. I could not believe Gabe actually filed for divorce while he was in a combat zone. I looked out the back sliding glass door then banged my head on it over and over as I wept. The physical pain was so much easier to deal with than the ache inside that I could not make go away.

When I composed myself enough, I sent my husband an e-mail. It said I couldn't believe he was doing this. I also threw in there that anyone with a little common sense knows you do not give a person bad news on a Friday. It increases the possibility of suicide. He e-mailed back and asked if I was planning on hurting myself. I told him that wasn't the point. I thought it was beyond inconsiderate of them to serve papers on a Friday. Not that a divorce is about being considerate.

I couldn't believe how easy the state of Wyoming made it for people to walk away from marriage. It truly saddened me. If I didn't fight or contest anything, it would have been over in three weeks like nothing ever happened. There was no way I would've made things that easy. I was determined to fight for my marriage somehow. I told my lawyer that I wanted to drag this on because I was not giving up on Gabe's and my relationship. I was also determined that my husband was going to face me if this was the way he wanted things to go. He couldn't just sit in another country and hire a lawyer to do his dirty work for him.

I screamed at my dad for not being there when I needed him most. I asked God why I had to go through this completely alone. Of course, as soon as I asked that, I heard, *You're not alone*, in my head. I knew God was with me, but I wanted to have someone physically there to hold me when I cried or needed a person to just listen.

I didn't need the Sunday school answers everyone kept giving me. I knew I should be in God's Word. I also was familiar with his promises that said he'd never leave me or forsake me. I didn't want anyone preaching to me. I *wanted* someone to truly and completely listen. No one could do that.

Everyone thought they needed to give me answers or solutions. So I cut myself off even more from those trying to help. I wouldn't answer the phone anymore unless I thought it was an emergency. I started ordering groceries online and looking for every excuse not to leave my house. I went to work and church. That was it—unless I absolutely had to get something from the store and couldn't wait.

I didn't make eye contact with others. If I saw someone I knew, I turned around and walked another direction. If I were a millionaire, I would have become a recluse like Howard Hughes did. People meant pain, and I did not want to add to the pain I was already feeling.

In May I found out I had multiple kidney stones. I was worried because the doctor said my symptoms could be caused by bladder cancer, but he needed to do an ultrasound to make sure. I needed lithotripsy, a medical procedure that used shock waves to break up the stones. The doctor told me he was going to electrocute me over two thousand times.

I sure didn't want to feel that. I was grateful he was going to give me medicine so that I would be knocked out during the event. My procedure was set for May 19. I wasn't thrilled about it, but it was better than having bladder cancer, so I counted my blessings. I was fine with dying, but a slow and painful death wasn't exactly what I was hoping for.

As I got close to the procedure date, I had to fill out paperwork for the hospital. I had another revelation while writing down the information. I had no emergency contact. There wasn't one person I wanted to put on the line. In that instant, I felt like an orphan. My family and friends were living all over the world. My mom and I were estranged at best. It was a revelation I could have done without.

"Do I *need* to put someone there?" I asked.

"We need someone in case something happens during the procedure."

I ended up putting an acquaintance from work. My dad was always my emergency contact or permanent address as I moved from state to state or country to country in the air force. When my husband and I got married, Gabe was my emergency contact, and my dad was my back up. I never put much thought into it before, but now it was like a neon sign in front of my face that I could not turn off.

The day of the procedure I had to ask someone from work to drive me and take me home since I was going to be drugged. I hated depending on anyone else like that. This frustration was partially because I was in Wyoming. If this were happening in Texas, it wouldn't have been an issue. I had a lot of friends and family there whom I could depend on. Little did I know the person I asked was only a few weeks from turning her back on me and letting me fall on my face when I needed help. This would just be the beginning of watching even my acquaintances abandon me.

The procedure went well, but when I woke up, I was in severe pain. When they put in or pulled out the tube in my throat, they ripped my throat up. I could hardly swallow, drink, or eat anything for the next two weeks because of the damage. I was so mad because they acted like it was normal. I've had a few surgeries and procedures and never had this problem before. It wasn't normal for my throat to burn when I drank water. Thankfully, my kidney stones were blown up and passing easily.

Besides work, I spent most of my time in June praying for my husband's safety and restoration of our marriage. He was due to come home from Afghanistan in July, but he wasn't telling me anything. He e-mailed I wasn't allowed to pick him up at the airport. Before he arrived, he had a coworker get his car from the house.

He was back about a week before I heard from him. I moved to a new townhome rental in May because I couldn't stand being in that house alone anymore. I was completely surprised by how passive aggressive my husband was during all of this.

He asked people to come pack up his stuff in the house so he didn't have to deal with me. His actions were another reason I wanted to make sure he had to face me if he wanted a divorce. I refused to make it easy. It wasn't like walking away from some high-school relationship. This was a marriage and a covenant with God! It was two souls being ripped apart after becoming one as God intended. There is a reason Scripture says, "So they are no longer two, but one flesh. Therefore what God has joined together, let no one separate" (Matthew 19:6, NIV).

I think another reason I was so hell-bent on saving my marriage was because I knew there wasn't anything I could do to bring my daddy back. No matter what, my dad was gone. But my husband was alive, and I could fight with every fiber of my being to save my marriage. Therefore, that was my plan.

The first time I saw him was July 10. He wanted to meet at a neutral location to exchange items that we still had of each other's. He brought his mom with him. She wouldn't speak to me or even look at me. I desperately wanted to confront her on actively pushing my husband to leave me. However, I knew I would not be able to act like a Christian if I did. So I didn't.

Gabe and I stood outside in the parking lot for over an hour talking. I asked him, "Did you ever love me since you were willing to leave so easily?"

"I did love you and always will." He leaned against my SUV and kicked around some loose pebbles.

"When I first saw you, it was so hard for me to keep from running to you and giving you a hug."

I kept my hands wrapped around my body but couldn't keep my eyes from his face. I wanted so badly to hold him and just feel his heart next to mine. "I miss you so much."

Before we separated, he agreed to meet for coffee the next morning to talk. "Can I have a hug?" I asked.

He took in a deep breath and then embraced me. It took everything I had to let him go. I bawled like a baby after he left.

Less than twenty-four hours later I sat across a table from him at Starbucks. We talked long past the morning rush had cleared out. I asked countless times, "What do I need to do so we can work on our marriage?"

He never gave me an answer. By the time my third cup of coffee was cold, I began crying.

"Let's go sit in your truck," he told me as he stood up. I didn't care if he just did it because he didn't want people to see me crying. It would be more private.

I threw my half-full drink into the trash and then walked through the door he held open for me. Once we were inside, I told him, "I just want one chance to make it up to you so I can show you I'm committed to our marriage."

He glanced at me once with this look in his eyes like he wanted to kiss me. I called him on it. "You totally want to kiss me," I said.

"Nah, I'm just full of caffeine." He tried to play it off but had a smile on his face.

I jumped on the chance, hoping that would help. We kissed, and I asked again, "Can we try to work on things?" I'll never forget his answer.

"I need to talk to my parents." I should have known at that moment my fighting would never amount to anything. He always needed his parents' approval. I got so excited and felt such hope in my heart even though I knew if his parents were the deciding factor we would never stand a chance. Then he didn't speak to me or reply to my texts for another two weeks. I felt like I was alone in the ocean treading water to stay alive. Once I finally glimpsed a ship in the distance, I slowly realized it turned out to only be my imagination.

Once he did finally call, we chatted off and on. Some days he would tell me we weren't going to get back together. Others he would consider it, and then we would spend time with each other and end up sleeping together. Eventually I went to his apartment to hang out and eat or just talk. When we were together in his home, we fell right back into our married ways. That is until late each evening when my coach turned back into a pumpkin, and I had to go back to my place.

After I returned from a TDY in Alabama for two weeks, I needed to talk to Gabe about some things I was considering. If he didn't want to work on our relationship, I needed to get away and focus on something else. I went to his apartment.

"I am considering volunteering for a three-hundred-sixty-five-day deployment to the Middle East. If there is even the smallest chance of us working on our marriage, I won't go." I wanted him to tell me where we stood, point-blank.

"You should go," he told me. "If I had the opportunity to leave Wyoming, I'd take it." It hurt terribly that he would say that. *How could he just quit and give up on our marriage as if it meant nothing?*

The next day I went into work and volunteered for a year in Afghanistan. Four short hours later I was accepted and given an official letter tasking me to Kandahar, Afghanistan. I didn't think it would happen that fast, but I was excited. The only problem was I would not leave until summer 2011. That was almost a year away.

I told Gabe immediately I was selected.

"Wow. I didn't think it would happen that fast."

His response aggravated me. "I gave you the power to stop me, but you didn't take it." *How could he be surprised about what happened when I warned him?*

In August, I went to the radiology clinic to have another ultrasound on my breasts. A week later they sent a letter saying I did not have breast cancer. I was grateful, but all I was truly worried about was saving my marriage. Gabe told me he was going TDY for three weeks to Albuquerque, New Mexico, for training.

Toward the end of August, my coworker and friend committed suicide. I knew he was having some trouble, but he never made it sound serious. He told me a few times he would get through it like everything else. I spoke to him the morning before he took his life. He came into my office and was smiling and had an upbeat attitude.

"Is there anything I can do to help?" I asked him.

"No, it'll be fine."

"If there is something I can do to help, even if it's just being there to talk, I am available any time," I told him before he left. There was nothing in his demeanor or attitude to suggest what he was considering. I replayed that conversation hundreds of times in my head to see if I missed anything or could have said something else. He went to lunch that day and never came back. I was devastated when I got the news. All I could think of was his young son he left behind.

I texted Gabe to let him know what happened and to tell him I wasn't taking the news very well. I wanted to talk about it in person and hopefully get a hug from the only person in Wyoming I trusted. He responded with a simple, cold text that read, "Sorry to hear that." Every time he would be cold, it crushed me. Over and over we went through the same routine. First, he treated me like a wife. Then he acted like I was only a distant relative. That left me feeling completely rejected.

A healthy person probably would have walked away, but I couldn't. There was part of me that felt I had to fight as hard as I could to save and restore my marriage. I knew there was nothing I could do to bring my daddy back. This was all I had left, and I despised the thought of another divorce. Another part of me felt as though I deserved the pain for what I did to my husband.

I was willing to endure any and all suffering he wanted to put me through after I hurt him so deeply. I sobbed many times while telling Gabe I would do anything to take all of his pain away. I never wanted to hurt the love of my life. I would've died for him to keep him from harm. Besides my dad, there was no one else I ever would have risked my life for out of unconditional love. I voluntarily joined the military, but there is a huge difference between fighting for freedom and being willing to lay down my life for my husband.

During the summer, I asked someone to snap my neck. I was completely serious and told them I would give them all of my dad's life insurance money if they would do it. The person declined. I did not care about anything anymore. In my mind, there was no reason at all for me to live. I couldn't offer the world anything. *What purpose could I possibly have now?* I'd lost everything important to me at once and did not want to live another day.

I had been fighting for months and looking for ways to stay married. I didn't want to give up and let him go. Everyone around me told me, "Just sign the divorce papers." On September 1, 2010, I gave in and wrote my signature on the documents. I shook the whole time. Afterward, I walked back out to my truck and cried.

Gabe was now TDY in Albuquerque. He asked me to come visit him for that weekend. I dropped everything, asked for leave, found someone to watch my dog, and bought a ticket to New Mexico. I looked at it as an opportunity to save our relationship and spend time with him without anyone else around.

We had an amazing weekend spending time together. I told him, "I regret signing the divorce papers. It ripped a hole in my soul. People were pushing me to change my name back to Castleberry, but I didn't want to."

As we were walking to the movies, he put his arm around me and said, "You don't have to change your name." Even the kind way he said it gave me hope. The last day we started out well, but then Gabe became very cold. We hardly spoke on the way to the airport. I asked for a hug when he dropped me off and cried when he left.

The Monday after I returned, our divorce was signed by the judge and was final. My heart sank when I saw the documents. Legally I couldn't call him my husband anymore. On paper, it looked like I'd lost the battle, but I refused to give up. My covenant of marriage with Gabe was to God, not man or the judicial system.

Shortly after our divorce was final, I felt that I needed to tell Gabe the whole story, that I felt forced into the situation with Marshall and that I felt I was protecting him by giving in. At first, he asked a few questions and then said I was lying. I told him very clearly that the only reason I was telling him now was because he wasn't my husband and he couldn't force me to report it. He didn't care about any of it, and he didn't want to discuss it any further.

Gabe went TDY to a conference over Halloween weekend then was sent TDY to school in Alabama for five and a half weeks. We texted occasionally while he was gone. A few days before he graduated SOS (Squadron Officer School), he texted and told me he missed me and wanted to see me when he got back.

I was overjoyed and couldn't wait to be near him again. Thursday, December 2, he returned. We saw each other and were intimate. For the first time I could ever remember, Gabe told me, "Your body is perfect."

That meant so much to me since it was just over a year before that he was constantly making comments about my pudgy belly. I felt like I had my husband back. He was proud of me again and attracted to me.

I didn't see him Friday because he hung out with a friend driving through from SOS. He invited me over on Saturday, although he was hung over from partying with his friend the night before. We spent time together a few days that week. It was comforting just sitting next to him on the couch studying. I was leaving for SOS soon, and I had one more test to take. While he typed on his computer, my feet were tucked under his leg to keep warm. It wasn't anything extravagant, but the closeness of it was everything to me.

That afternoon we made love before I left to get ready for my wing holiday party on base. When I was getting ready to leave, he jokingly made a comment about me being a booty call. I was livid and could not believe *the man* I had defended to everyone was acting like *every other man* in my life. I was angry and brokenhearted he would ever make a joke or statement like that.

I went home and got ready for the gathering. I got to the party around seven and socialized as best I could, still being upset about Gabe's comment. While dancing with a guy friend, a woman came in between us, trying to make a point. For some reason, this bothered me more than usual. Instead of just getting angry and walking away, I pushed her across the dance floor. She had a look in her eyes of total shock.

"You messed with the wrong person," I told her. As I walked away, I kept replaying it in my head. What in the world made me so mad that I crossed that line? Never in my life had I done that before. I had arguments with people. However, I never actually laid my hands on someone in an aggressive manner with every intention of taking it to the next level.

I decided it was best that I go home and not go out after the base party. I went home and parked my truck in the garage.

7:03 a.m.

But when I am afraid, I will put my trust in you.
I praise God for what he has promised. I trust
in God, so why should I be afraid? What can
mere mortals do to me?

Psalm 56:3-4 (NLT)

I was going on leave for two weeks, and I could not wait
to head out. I took Gabe the birthday and Christmas
presents I bought him. After I handed them to him,
I said, "I'm sorry for ruining our relationship. Please
forgive me." We had a short conversation that left our
relationship without any new developments. I wished
him the best and told him happy birthday.

I started driving to Texas. I begged God to help me
get over Gabe. My feelings hurt and caused so much
pain. If it wasn't His plan for Gabe's and my relationship to be restored, I needed help to let him go. I
thought of the movie *Bruce Almighty*. Jennifer Aniston's
character is crying in bed begging God to help her stop
loving Jim Carey's character. I've done that hundreds of
times, but it wasn't working.

God, Please help my broken heart heal. I do well
for a few days, and then I'm right back to missing him and wanting my marriage back. If it is in
your plan for us not to get back together, please

help me get past this. Please heal his heart, Lord.
I love and miss him so much.

I want to focus my life…on you…and fall in
love with you like I've never known. I want you
to complete my life like everyone talks about. I
want you to be my everything so I'm not con-
sumed with anything else. You are my purpose
and my salvation. Praise and glory be to you
alone. Amen.

I was going on leave for two weeks in Texas and
then heading to Alabama for five and a half weeks of
Squadron Officer School (SOS). I knew this would not
be easy. I always did well for a week or two. Then I
would start missing Gabe and text him.

Another difficulty would be spending Christmas in
the Lone Star state. It would be the first time I went
home since Dad's funeral. I was anxious, angry, and
confused the whole drive home. I just wanted out of
Cheyenne and to be close to my friends. I needed my
support network so I could take some time for myself
to heal and not worry about work or any other issues.

I was still begging God to take my life. Every time
I drove in the snow, I waited to hit black ice so I could
just be done with all the pain. I had no fear and didn't
care what happened to me. That was a very dangerous
place for me to be.

I arrived at my godmother's home on December
20. When I woke up the next morning, I was very
depressed even though it was my birthday.

This was my first one without Daddy calling me at
exactly 7:03 a.m. to tell me happy birthday. He phoned

me every year at that time because that was when I was born. It was our special thing, and it meant more to me than any present ever could.

The first text message I received for my birthday was from Gabe, which surprised me. It was those sorts of gestures that kept me holding on to our relationship and yet continually shattered my heart as well. I sent a reply text thanking him but didn't hear back.

I spent time with friends but was dreading Christmas. I most feared the pain and emotions that were inevitable for my first Christmas without my daddy and my husband. Although I wasn't alone, I may as well have been. No one could help me with the emptiness inside no matter how much they wanted to.

Once I woke up Christmas morning, I texted Gabe to wish him a merry Christmas. Next I prayed for God's strength to help me through the day and my relationship with Gabe.

> Abba, please restore my marriage. Abba God Almighty, please forgive me for failing you. Help me forgive those who fail me. I know you understand my pain, hurt, and loneliness. I also know you have a plan for everything. Help me to press through this dark hour with your strength and grace. I want to bring glory to you. Jesus, I continue to lift up Gabe and our marriage to you. I'm asking for a miracle to bring us back together and glorify your name.

> I love you and praise your holy name. Abba, I ask all these things in the name of Jesus Christ, my Savior! Amen.

I am so blessed to have them in my life!

I went into the living room to spend time with my godmother, Taylor (her son I call my brother), and her husband, Dick. I knew they did their best to make me feel like one of the family. As grateful as I was for their thoughtfulness, it was still a difficult day, to say the least. I ended up spending three or four hours in bed that afternoon. As much as I wanted to be okay, I was depressed and couldn't fight it or hide it from those around me.

While I was home in Texas, I worked on getting Dad's house sold and looked for another one. I loved the land he had. However, I couldn't go to his place, much less stay in it. After looking at a handful of houses, I actually found one I loved. It was around the corner from my godmother's. I planned on using the profits from Dad's house as a down payment on the new house. The whole process was bittersweet.

I enjoyed my time with friends and getting away from work even though it was a painful time. On my drive to Alabama for SOS, I continued crying out to God.

> Jesus, I need your help because I'm not sure I have truly grieved my daddy. I have been so consumed with saving my marriage and trying to prove to Gabe I was dedicated and committed. I have not been able to go through the mourning process. I don't want this to become an obstacle later in life. I need to mourn the loss of my daddy so I can then completely grieve the end of my marriage. I love you and need you to help me through this. In Jesus's glorious name, amen.

In January I drove to Alabama to start SOS. Initially, I had no desire to interact with people in my class. I wanted to just get through it. After the first week, that plan didn't happen...and I'm glad. I met some great people and started having a blast while hanging out with them.

We worked on class projects, went to dinner, grabbed drinks, and got to know each other. I made a few new friends and ended up having an amazing time. We ended up doing well as a team and won multiple awards. Our focus was always on having fun as a group. After graduating from SOS, I drove back to Cheyenne, Wyoming, and returned to work.

A week later I noticed I hadn't had a period since December. It was the second week of February, and I should have started already. Even though I doubted it, I took a pregnancy test out of curiosity. Of all the days for me to take the test, it was February 12, 2011—exactly one year after my dad suddenly left me.

Three minutes later I almost passed out. For the first time in my life and after months of Gabe and I trying to get pregnant while we were married, the stick said it'd finally happened. My first thought was, *How in the world will I tell Gabe? How will he react? How bad will his reaction hurt me this time?*

I asked God, "Is this supposed to be funny?" Between finding out I was pregnant on the one-year anniversary of my daddy's passing and the fact that my ex-husband was not speaking to me, I didn't know how I would deal with this. I was terrified to tell Gabe. I grieved the thought of having a baby without my dad being part of his or her life.

I sent him a text with a picture of the pregnancy test that indicated I was pregnant. I knew he would question me. During our texting back and forth, he insinuated that I was a liar. He made it clear that he didn't want anything to do with the baby.

It was crushing to my soul that he acted that way. I took more tests to make sure it wasn't a false positive. Every test, day or night, was positive. It was like the scene out of *Knocked Up* where Alison buys dozens of pregnancy tests and takes them over and over. To those on the outside it would be humorous but would be beyond frightening to the person taking the test. Next I went to a women's clinic in Denver to get an ultrasound and to verify it was true.

The doctor said, "You are pregnant, but it does not appear to be viable. I want you to come back in another week so I can check on things."

I didn't want to go through this alone, and Gabe wasn't any help because he refused to speak to me. I contacted my godmother and asked if she could fly out for a few days. She agreed. While together, I told her, "I need to do something to take my mind off what is coming."

We went to the mall for retail therapy. Blowing through thousands of dollars and drinking was quickly becoming my Band-Aid for the pain. I spent a very pretty penny on my Rolex watch. While it was beautiful, it never fixed the pain I felt going through a miscarriage.

We went back to the doctor together. On February 18, they induced the miscarriage. I was given a picture from the ultrasound that I will always keep. I miscarried our baby on February 22, Gabe's and my anniversary of all days. I knew I wasn't supposed to question God's plan, but I couldn't help but wonder why things happened on their particular dates. They already meant something, whether good or bad. I texted Gabe and told him I was having a miscarriage but not the details behind it. He didn't reply or ask any questions.

While dealing with that loss, I learned something about my mother. When I talked with her, I found out she had lung cancer. Instead of being in regular contact with her or just writing her a large check, I tried to help in another way.

I assisted her side of the family by providing them with information on how to get the process for grants for her medical bills started. I guess that wasn't good enough, though. Her older brother told me, "Since she's your mom, it's your job to take care of her." Unless I handed them cash or a check, they figured I wasn't doing my part. I didn't take that very well and spoke even less to my mother and her side of the family after that.

I did my best to stay focused at work. At first, things were going well. I received very good feedback from my commander.

"You exceeded in nearly every area, but everyone needs to continue to work to improve," she stated as I sat in her office.

No one is perfect, but I felt I was doing pretty well. I knew where she wanted me to progress. Two weeks later it all changed. Without warning, the same Commander called me to her office.

When I walked in, she said, "You are not going to expect what is coming. You are required to have a mental-health evaluation." She read about two pages worth of details, but I blacked out and don't remember anything past "mental health evaluation."

She then proceeded to tell me the first sergeant and chief would be following me home to take my weapons and ammunitions away from me.

If this had taken place shortly after returning from my dad's funeral, this would have made sense. I had many suicidal thoughts that I didn't hide from anyone. *But why are they concerned now?*

I was so angry, frustrated, and confused as to why after such great feedback I was being forced to go to mental health. I received no warning and no explanation. To me that meant communication failed somewhere. Little did I know this would be the beginning of the end of my air force career.

not what I've done but what I've overcome

I have told you these things, so that in Me you may have [perfect] peace and confidence. In the world you have tribulation and trials and distress and frustration; but be of good cheer [take courage; be confident, certain, undaunted]! For I have overcome the world. [I have deprived it of power to harm you and have conquered it for you.]

John 16:33 (AMP)

I was followed home by the first sergeant and the group chief after my meeting with the commander. I prayed during the whole drive. I couldn't understand what was possibly going on. I kept asking God to help me control my anger and keep my mouth shut. I thought about all that I had been through in my life. I have come to realize that everything happens for a reason.

Jeremiah 29:11 (NIV) echoed in my head like a fire truck siren approaching danger:

"For I know the plans I have for you," declares the LORD, "plans to prosper you and not to harm you, plans to give you hope and a future."

Throughout the last year and this car ride, I held on tightly to this verse. Another one that I repeated to myself as I stopped at a red light was Genesis 50:20 (NLT):

> You intended to harm me, but God intended it all for good. He brought me to this position so I could save the lives of many people.

I turned onto my street. I knew whatever might come my way, God intended it for my good and his glory. It was *not* about me! It will never be about what I can do but what I can do with Christ's strength in me.

I never thought I would survive my dad's death. Had it been up to me, I wouldn't have, but God carried me through the pain of simultaneously losing him and my husband forsaking me in my darkest hour. I understood he wouldn't abandon me now. Daily I gave my life and issues to him and tried not to take back the control I wanted him to have. He had the perfect plan, and I just needed to follow Proverbs 3:5 (AMP):

> Lean on, trust in, and be confident in the Lord with all your heart and mind and do not rely on your own insight or understanding.

My .20-gauge shotgun my daddy gave me for protection, my 1911 Sig Sauer .45, and all of my ammunition was taken. I was livid to say the least. That week I met with mental health. I kept my arms crossed the entire time, not attempting to hide my unhappiness about being there.

"You are here so that I can assess if you are okay and mentally healthy enough to carry a weapon. I've been briefed on what you went through in the past year."

I knew he wasn't fully aware of the situation. Someone made it look like this was simply disguised to ensure I was sound before heading out on my deployment. I was skeptical about what was going on and paranoid something was about to go bad. My commander signed off on me volunteering for the 365 the previous year while I was going through my hardest times. If she was concerned about my health, this should have been done then.

The health assessment I took on the computer showed I was paranoid when people were around me. After seeing that, I thought, *If you knew everything I'd been through, can you really blame me for not trusting people?*

"You're fine," the counselor said during our final meeting. "I found you fit to deploy and carry weapons with no concern."

This was not a shock to me since I knew I was much better now than a year ago. I thought about an unresolved issue and wondered if it was the cause of this hassle.

I'd been having a problem with a particular second lieutenant talking unprofessionally about me to subordinates. It was brought to my attention by multiple people, including one who was very reliable. I confronted the slandering woman.

"If you have a problem with me, you need to address it with *me*, not our subordinates." I kept my head high and spoke with authority.

"*Who* told you I said something?" she asked, more concerned with who said it than anything else. She looked up momentarily, probably mentally narrowing her suspect list.

"I don't care if you like me as a person. At work, we need to keep things professional and courteous." I hoped I got my point across without divulging who my informants were.

Nothing changed. I continued to hear what she said about me. I sent her an e-mail stating she needed to come to me directly and not to other people if she had a problem with me. I again reminded her that at work she needed to remember her customs and courtesies and keep things professional.

Oddly, the day I sent the e-mail, my commander told me I needed to back off our lieutenants for a while. I was completely floored. I told her exactly what was going on with this specific situation.

"I'm trying to handle it professionally and at the lowest level." I avoided mentioning the issue to my supervisor up until this point. I knew she had more important things to worry about.

"Would you like me to sit down with both of you and act as a mediator?"

"She and I are adults. We *should* be able to take care of it without a mediator."

Obviously I didn't understand exactly what was going on behind my back. Next thing I knew the Commander took away my job and responsibilities then moved me to another location. From that moment on, I haven't had a productive job, and I could tell something more was going on. I sat in different offices doing busy work, causing me to go stir-crazy. I felt like a high school kid going through in-school suspension.

I was dually hated in my two jobs as the manpower and personnel flight commander and the operations officer for the squadron before this not-so-subtle change. I was taken from jobs that kept me busy and put in a location where there was hardly anything productive to do. The commander then started an investigation on me and still kept me in the dark about what exactly was going on.

There was a voice in my head telling me another possibility. Maybe the rumors about the guy I cheated on my husband with were taken directly to the commander. No one had any physical proof of anything that happened, not even my ex-husband. However, in the air force, it's all about perception…including rumors.

F. E. Warren AFB was worse than being in high school. Rumors ran rampant because the OPS TEMPO (operations tempo) was slow and people got bored easily. From the moment my husband and I arrived rumors were flying around about me. Every time I turned around I was supposedly having sex with someone else, and according to the rumor mill they were all enlisted.

That was one of the many reasons I despised the assignment. I preferred locations like my last assignment. It had a fast pace, true wartime mission, and constant deployments. I thrived on being busy and feeling like I had a purpose.

I contacted Gabe. "Are you part of the investigation against me?"

"What are you talking about?" he said in a scruffy voice over the phone.

"So you don't know anything about it?" I questioned him further.

"No one's been asking me about anything."

That's when I knew the second lieutenant was sticking her head where she shouldn't have. It was one thing if my ex-husband wanted to end my career, but not someone else who didn't have actual details or proof of anything. I was furious to say the least.

"Gabe, you could be called in and questioned about us." I needed to give him a heads-up.

"What?"

I heard him exhale loudly. I could understand him being unhappy about being forced into this. We ended our conversation a few minutes later.

After a few weeks in one unproductive "job," I was moved to another area. I was now *working* (I use that word loosely) in the Commander's Action Group at the 20th Numbered Air Force for a two-star general. I assisted with tasks coming down from our major command (MAJCOM). I spent the majority of the time looking for jobs on the outside and surfing the Internet. We didn't have many taskers (responsibilities to attend to) come in. Even when a few would, after five minutes, I'd completed what was needed.

I told my commander on multiple occasions, "I'm bored and not really being utilized." I hated life more and more every day.

"I'll see what I can do." That's what she said but not what she did. It seemed like she told me what I wanted to hear and then ignored the issue and never let me know what was going on. All I heard were rumors and that it shouldn't take long for everything to be complete.

Weeks of waiting for the investigation to be over turned into months. I lost all hope in the air force. I was completely miserable and hated life more than I thought possible. They took someone with pride, love, and respect for their job and flipped them 180 degrees! I had officially lost everything as far as I was concerned—my dad, my husband, and now my career. For an officer in today's air force, there is no recovering from something like this. It didn't matter if they couldn't find any evidence. I knew I was done. At the end of April, my commander gave me a no contact order with Gabe. She made it sound like he requested it. I was hurt but angrier that he did it.

> God, I know things take time, and I know you have things I need to learn. I feel like a slow learner right now. I have no idea which direction my life is going. I miss Daddy so stinking much. Gabe still has a strong hold on my heart, and I don't know

how long it is going to take me to move forward. I passed him yesterday leaving base, and my heart sank. I felt so much pain. I have never loved anyone I was in a relationship with like him. I gave myself entirely to him.

I know I need to rely on you and only you. This is a very difficult lesson for me. I know I'm a control freak, and I know I used to lean on Daddy and Gabe for everything. I'm not sure about any other lesson I was supposed to learn through all of these losses over the last year, but I know leaning solely on you is number one. I give you my heart and my life daily. I want you to lead me in every step I take. I know I will take control from time to time, but you are the one with the perfect plan. I will continue to surrender my life to you daily.

I'm so tired of the pain. I do not trust anyone around me at work, and that is taking a toll on me. God, please help me find at least *one* person that is not out for themselves. Otherwise, please help the time pass quickly so I can go on my deployment and get away from this place.

I love you, and I am trying to lean not on my own understanding but on yours alone. Thank you, Jesus, for dying on the cross for my sins. Thank you for saving my soul, for your grace, for your mercy, for your forgiveness, and your unconditional love. Thank you for carrying me more than I have walked since last February. I would not be here without you.

All of these things in your holy name, amen.

Throughout this ordeal, I e-mailed friends and posted my thoughts and feelings on Facebook without reservation. I was shocked at one comment from a supposed friend in April. A couple days later I responded with this note:

> Wow, I have been blown away by people's reactions over the last fifteen months of my life. I think I heard the true kicker recently when a *friend* wrote, "I unfriended you on here because I cannot deal with the pain you are feeling."
>
> Um, okay…try actually going through it for the last fifteen months! My goodness, I am sorry if the pain I am going through and dealing with daily is too much for you to hear about. The shock I felt when I read that was indescribable.
>
> I know that I have posted very personal things on here, and I know that some people cannot understand. I get that, but it is my personal mess that I am going through. Please keep in mind a few things: my page is private and only my friends can see anything I post or publish on Facebook. I, honest to God, *do not* have any of my *best* friends here or close for me to talk to. This is the best therapy for me right now because I hate talking on the phone. I have gone to counseling, and it just aggravates me.
>
> I truly feel like every time I start to get a grip on everything something else happens. This is the best I know how to deal with everything. I will not apologize for being completely open and honest. Would it be any different if I wrote a

book about everything to help others and made money off it? Would that be okay? I don't know what people expect from me, but I have lost and experienced more than I would wish on a person in one life, much less a year.

Yes, there is always someone worse off than where you stand…maybe I am that person for you. If someone is truly going through a lot more than me, I lift that person up in prayer because I cannot imagine surviving much more.

There is no doubt in my mind that Christ has been carrying me since the day my husband, the love of my life, told me he wanted a divorce. Then three days later my daddy, my world, died unexpectedly. Don't worry. I will not list everything else that I have dealt with, but I know by the grace of *God* alone I am here today. For what reason, I still do not know, but "if only for the one," as my church says. One of these days I may understand what all of this is for. But until then, I will do my best to focus on God and live my life accordingly.

If you are one of the people who cannot handle to hear my cries, please unfriend me as well. God bless you and keep you safe always,

Tiffany Dawn Castleberry

I needed a break and to get away from all the backstabbers and liars around me in Wyoming. I took leave over the Memorial Day weekend for ten days. I decompressed in Texas with my godmother and close friends. I needed to find a healthy way to mourn Daddy passing away, Gabe leaving me abruptly, the reality of my career going down in flames, and learning my mom had cancer and how that truly affected me. I knew all of this stress was taking a toll on my body because my hair was falling out nearly in handfuls, my face was a teenage nightmare of acne, and my body was as tightly wound as a child's music box.

I felt like an entirely different person while I was home on leave. The people I was around loved me and wanted to support me. No one was out to get me. Even my godmother said I looked so much happier while I was there.

I woke up, went out on the patio, and listened to the water nearby and birds. I sat there and felt at peace while taking in God's beautiful creations. I thanked him for the ability to appreciate where I was at that moment. It was my quiet time to pray, be still, listen, and remember the blessings I still had. I would cry over many things and beg God to help me survive. Those mornings helped me fall in love with my new house I'd purchased. I wanted to be home instead of in the military. It was the first time I felt like I belonged there instead of in the air force.

I would have left my career in a split second to save my marriage if Gabe ever wanted me to. Usually a few days or maybe one week into leave I was ready to get back to work. This time was completely different because I didn't want to return. I experienced peace about leaving the military and going home to start anew. In fact, I dreaded the thought of going back to Wyoming and dealing with fake people only out for themselves. I knew that was God's way of letting me know things were changing, and my future wasn't what *I* had planned.

God was making me into a new creation in him, and I was slowly starting to notice the changes. They included my attitude first and foremost but also consisted of my desires and where I wanted to be. Don't get me wrong. I still had moments when I would rather strangle someone than love them, but I wasn't acting so aggressively anymore. God was showing me I was not *what I had done* in my past but that it was about *what I had overcome* through his love, grace, mercy, and forgiveness!

It had been a turbulent fifteen months, but God was making major changes in me. I would never be the woman I was before February 2010. I would forever be stronger and less naive. There was a new yearning in my heart to do something I loved and was passionate about rather than having a job to pay the bills.

Around the time of my leave from work, my zeal was changing. It wasn't the air force anymore. I used to be so proud of my job and looked forward to the next challenge. After all that had happened I was surrounded by people I would never trust in a war zone, and that spoke volumes. If I could not trust someone to have my back in combat, I would not work with that individual at home base. It was time to move on. That trip home was everything I needed to decompress.

Toward the end of my vacation, Gabe contacted me through Facebook and asked how I was doing. This caught me off guard because of the no-contact order.

I didn't understand why he would ask for this or what I had done to get it. I messaged him, asking, "Why did you request the no-contact order?"

He wrote back, "I didn't know we had a no-contact order. Is it still in effect?"

"It ended a couple of days ago. How was it possible you didn't know? I was told you requested it." I exhaled while I typed.

"I truly wasn't aware of it at all." I imagined him typing on his laptop sitting on his couch, where I wanted to be.

"Why did you contact me?" I wrote. I needed to know where our relationship was headed. This going back and forth was killing me. I thought if I wasn't allowed to contact him for thirty days, it might help break that cycle.

"I'm used to hearing from you at least once a week." His words made him seem concerned. I went back and forth between joy at his care and frustration at having feelings for him.

"I wanted to see if you were okay. How's your mom's cancer?" I'd let him know about it shortly after I found out myself.

"Last I heard, my mother is cancer free but will continue to get checkups regularly. That's because she still has a mass in her lung."

After some going back and forth, I wrote, "I don't have your number. If you want to chat, you should text me." Then I realized not only had I deleted his number, but I had gotten a new number for my phone since the last time we talked. I was actually trying to cut ties for my own sake, but that wasn't working.

right back where I shouldn't be

For I do not do the good I want to do, but the evil I do not want to do—this I keep on doing.

Romans 7:19 (NIV)

We exchanged the information. Shortly after the e-mailing through Facebook, we started texting. I wrote him that I bought a house in Texas on the lake and sent him pictures. We were getting along pretty well for a change.

The day after I returned, I was scheduled to have surgery on my wrist to remove a ganglion cyst. I had to have someone pick me up since I was being sedated or the hospital wouldn't release me. I told Gabe about this. We were both still stationed in Cheyenne. He worked at the Guard Base while I worked at the AFB. At this time, I found out since January he'd been living in Fort Collins, Colorado. I was shocked but let it slide.

I texted, "Would you mind picking me up from the hospital? I'm having surgery in Fort Collins, and I couldn't find anyone to do it."

He didn't respond right away, so I wrote more. "I wouldn't ask if I had friends here, but I don't."

"Yeah, okay. But I'll be late because I have to work," he texted back.

On the day of the surgery, Gabe arrived to get me. It was the first time I had seen him in over six months. When he came around the corner, my insides lit up like a Christmas tree. I tried to hide it on the outside. I missed him so much.

I started to walk after I picked up my backpack. He grabbed it to carry it for me. I was shocked he was being so nice. I told him, "I can carry it myself since it would be on my shoulder. I only had surgery on my wrist."

"I insist," he said.

Of course my heart melted. Here was the man I loved treating me like he had when we were dating.

After we walked out of the hospital, he looked at me. "It's really good to see you," he stated, and then he embraced me in a hug. "You look beautiful."

I was done and right back where I shouldn't be: madly in love with my ex-husband and wanting him back. It wasn't like I ever really stopped feeling that way, but I had stuffed those feelings down inside and was doing well at ignoring them. As we walked to his vehicle, I was looking for his blue Honda Accord.

"I got a new truck," he said as he pointed to his black Toyota 4 Runner. He had told me many times he always wanted one. The odd thing to me was it was black and not white. Every time Gabe talked about getting a vehicle, he almost always said he loved white. I told him I thought black made vehicles look sharper. I doubt what I said had anything to do with his decision, but it was in my thought process when I saw it.

We went to dinner in his new large toy. Of course, it didn't take long for me to start crying. I told him, "It may be easy for you to do this, but it is still very hard for me to just act like we are friends." Everything inside of me wanted to jump over the table, hold him close to me, and never let go. We ate a good dinner, and our conversation was friendly when I wasn't in tears.

Afterward, he asked, "Do you want to come over?"

I thought about it for a moment. I knew if I went back to his place we would end up having sex. I would feel used again. So I told him, "I need to get back and feed Missy, so just take me to my truck." It was so hard for me not to go with him, but I was trying to be good.

He returned me to my vehicle in the hospital parking lot. "Thank you for picking me up and for dinner," I told him before I opened the door. After a quick hug, I got out. It didn't take long after driving off before I started crying again. It was as though my heart broke every time I left him. I never experienced feeling as if someone was a part of my soul like Gabe. To me, it was akin to our souls united when we were together. When I left him, they were ripped apart all over again.

On the way home, I cried to God, asking him, "Why don't I deserve a second chance? God, I just want my husband back!"

I texted Gabe and told him it was very hard for me to leave and not give him a kiss. He replied and said he thought about it too. I returned to work the next day and was asked to prove I had surgery. I did it, but I was agitated. I had never just disappeared from work without my supervisor/commander knowing. Having a desk job with a wrist that was just cut open was difficult. Typing was a nightmare at the beginning, but since I didn't have too much "work" to do, I managed.

That weekend Gabe invited me to go swimming at his apartment. I was excited to spend time with him but more joyful about him seeing me in a bikini. I had been working out very hard, and my stomach was flat and getting toned.

I got to his apartment and had one of his special margaritas. We walked to the swimming pool. I disrobed and waited to see his reaction. It didn't take long before he mentioned, "You look great."

His compliments meant the world to me after he seemed so unhappy with my body while we were married. We lay out for a while and then chose to get in the water to cool off. Gabe got in first, and then I did after the chill subsided. After I was in the water, he came up behind me, wrapped his arms around me, and kissed the top of my head.

I smiled from ear to ear and soaked in every moment. We talked about different things and life when we were married. We were laughing and having a good time. He held me close and called me "Babe." Every time he did, I felt like a schoolgirl who'd just learned her crush reciprocated the feelings. He was the love of my life, and no matter how much he hurt me, I had forgiven him as Christ forgave me. I just wanted my husband back.

We went back to lie out for a little bit longer. I began the conversation. "Do you ever think about us getting back together?" I was staring up at a cloud that looked like a teddy bear. I didn't want to make eye contact when he answered.

"I do, but I wonder if you would mess up again after ten years or so."

My heart felt squeezed. I understood his fears. "I swear on everything sacred I would never do that again. I would never do anything to jeopardize our relationship." I left the subject alone after that.

We decided to go back to his apartment since we ran out of margaritas. It didn't take long before we were making love in his bedroom. After all of the sexual abuse in my life, Gabe was the only person I enjoyed being with. I felt that was God's way of telling me this was one of many reasons why our relationship was meant to be. For a person with a lot of sexual abuse in her past who hated sex and viewed it as barbaric, the fact that I actually enjoyed making love to Gabe spoke volumes.

There is a quote from the movie *Forces of Nature* that captures how I felt: "I always thought sex was a horrible obligation God put on women. Like cramps or high heels."

From the moment I first had sex, I loathed it and found it painful every time. It was as if I was a piece of meat that was only there to satisfy someone else's desires. With Gabe, it was different from the very beginning. He was concerned about how I felt and would ask if I was okay. He was always gentle with me and very loving. I wasn't in pain, uncomfortable, or treated disrespectfully. We fit perfectly together, and it was the first time I wanted to work hard on viewing sex the way God intended. I wanted it to be special, spiritual, and intimate. The problem was I didn't know how to change years of negative thoughts into positive thoughts. All I knew was with Gabe it was always unique.

We spent more time with each other and went to grab some food before I headed back to Cheyenne for the night. Our relationship picked back up. Our time together after that weekend increased. We went to the movies and often hung out. We still had hiccups occasionally because he never could understand the damage done to me before him.

Some days were better than others, but I was holding on with everything I had. I constantly prayed for God to work on Gabe's heart...along with his parents'.

We were texting one night. Out of the blue, he sent a text to me that read, "We need to get together before I leave for Korea."

I texted back and wrote, "*What?*" He quickly responded that the message was meant for his cousin. He'd intended on telling me to my face. I burst into tears. He wrote asking if I was okay, and I told him I was crying and wasn't taking the news very well.

He texted me to come spend the night with him, and we would talk about it. I ran upstairs, got my stuff together, and made sure my dog, Missy, had water and food. I left the back door open for her and then took off for Colorado. All I could think about on the way was how much that cut our time together and would make it more difficult for me to prove to him we could work on our relationship. I was praying and asking God to help us utilize the remaining months we had before he left to rebuild our trust and friendship.

When I got there, Gabe was a little intoxicated and in a good mood. We talked on the couch for a little bit, and he lay down with his legs across my lap. I loved when he did that while we talked. That was peaceful to me.

"What do you think about me leaving?" he asked me.

"It really upset me."

"You volunteered for a yearlong deployment," he replied.

"I asked you first, and you told me to go," I quickly reminded him.

"I didn't ask for this. It just happened."

I understood, but it still didn't comfort me. "My fear is if I can't get you to trust me when we are in the same country, would you even try if we are that far apart?" The thought of being without him nearly killed me, but the idea of not being in the same country terrified me.

We went to sleep and even cuddled for a while, which was surprising to me. Usually when we shared the same bed, I would give him as much space as I could. This time was different. All night he would roll over and kiss me on the cheek or head and hug me. It was so sweet, and I thought something was changing between us. Maybe he was ready to give us another chance.

After we got up the next morning, we went to breakfast. I went to use the restroom when he put our name on the list. A minute after I returned, the hostess called out, "Walker, party of two."

My heart skipped a beat. He probably didn't think twice about it, but it had been a long time since I'd heard that. It surprised me because he usually used his first name if asked.

We went on spending time together for a while, but he went back and forth between being sweet and cold. I just kept praying for God to sort it out.

In late June I was called in by the investigating officer for an interview. I finally found out what the allegations were against me. The charges were fraternization, adultery, abuse of rank, AWOL, and giving orders in the commander's name without the commander's knowledge.

I expected the fraternization and adultery, even though the military doesn't really go after adultery anymore. The rest of it was a load of crap. I had no idea where anyone could have come up with that garbage. My next thought was, *If anyone is going to say I was AWOL, it should be my supervisor, which is my commander, not a subordinate!*

The only allegation they had even a hint of evidence on was fraternization. I was ready to take full responsibility and accept any punishment they wanted to give me within reason. I never tried to get out of anything. I just wasn't happy about how it was brought about.

The investigating officer turned in his report to the JAG office. They told him it was insufficient. I thought, *If there wasn't evidence, what do you expect?* I knew then that something smelled badly and this wasn't going to end easily.

With the report turned in to JAG, I asked for my weapons back. I received them and my ammunition after a couple of days. I then started asking my ADC (Area Defense Council) when things should be wrapping up. Most people expected it to be soon, although they had been saying that since it began. I hoped to be out by the fall or end of the year at the latest.

In July, my commander had her Change of Command ceremony. I made sure to go so I could apologize to her for how the last six months had turned out. I never intended on making things difficult for her and was sorry for not handling things better so we didn't have to go through this.

"Thank you for what you taught me while you were here and for helping me become a better officer."

She gave me a hug and told me, "If you ever need me, don't hesitate to contact me."

My new commander pulled me from 20th NAF and brought me back to the FSS (Force Support Squadron) to work. With everything going on, I was surprised he wanted me there. However, I told him, "I will do whatever you need me to do." I wanted to move past everything that was going on. I knew I had to prove myself to him because he didn't know anything about me besides what he learned from the investigation.

I told him from the beginning that I would like to believe I could move past this and finish my career. I was a realist, though, and knew the air force was looking to get rid of people. With one mess up, I would be gone. I also let him know, "I have no problem with that, and I would prefer it to be sooner rather than later."

There was no question what I wanted: to be out of that place. I desired to get back to Texas to be near my mom if she passed away. I wanted my support system. Therefore, I started focusing on going home and what that would mean.

carried by the lord

I will be your God throughout your lifetime-
-until your hair is white with age. I made you,
and I will care for you. I will carry you along
and save you.

Isaiah 46:4 (NLT)

Toward the end of August, I wrote Gabe a letter.

I am not well. I have completely lost myself over
the last nineteen months trying to make sense
of losing Dad and you. All I have been doing is
trying to figure out ways to better myself and
save us. I am going crazy inside myself. I have
done everything you wanted by changing how
I eat, cooking and not eating out, how I do the
house work, changing how I dress, wearing
makeup, working out more, and deepening my
relationship with God.

Unfortunately, I could make myself into the
woman you have dreamed of, and I don't think
it would matter. Whatever your mom said to
you in that letter last year made up your mind
for you. A day or two before you got the letter I
was the love of your life, your one and only "no
matter what," and I was not perfect, but I was
perfect for you. That letter changed everything,

and I have no idea what she even said. I know you haven't completely let me go, or you would not go back and forth like you do.

For my own sanity, I cannot do this anymore. I love you more than I have ever loved anyone. I gave myself entirely to you, which I have never done before. I have fought for you longer and harder than anyone in my life. I have been willing to be and/or do anything to save us and prove my unconditional love for you. I have sworn on everything sacred and important to me that I would never screw up again and I would make you the happiest person in the world if given the chance.

I have done everything I possibly could at the sake of losing myself. The Sunday you stayed the night, I realized I couldn't do it anymore. That's why I was a babbling idiot. You say you don't want to hurt me and it's not just about making love, but I'm not sure. Gabe, I have been willing to go through all of the pain and suffering you think I deserve because I know I hurt you and I did a horrible thing.

At what point is it enough though? If you don't want to hurt me, why do you keep playing with my emotions? I have not hidden my intentions or how I feel from you. I want you back! I have told you that when you hold me, make love to me, and tell me you miss me it gives me hope for us. If you don't want there to ever be an "us," you have to stop.

I am not well, and I need professional help, which I am getting. I have beaten myself and created insane stories my whole life to get attention when things didn't go my way or I couldn't handle the trauma. At the hazard of my own life, I have turned myself inside out to please you and get you back. You have lived a near perfect life and will never completely understand what I have been through or what it has done to me.

I need help, and I need to fix me. I don't know if you were ever truly willing to help me get better or be there for me while I got therapy for all of my issues. I tried to tell you in Afghanistan that I have issues I need to work through…like intimacy. *I am damaged!* As much as I have tried to fix things myself, it is time for me to admit I cannot do it alone. I need to be completely honest about who I am and what I do to myself.

The church sermon changed everything last week. Sunday was the first day I was completely honest about what I've done in my life. I don't know if anyone will be able to accept what I have done and love me through God's eyes, but I have to do this for me or things will start getting much worse.

I am at my absolute worst right now. All I have wanted was to have the opportunity to make you happy and get my life back on track. This last time of us being together and you ignoring me again has sent me into a tailspin. Before I do something more stupid than what I have already done, I need to get help. I am taking off my mask and being honest about who I am and what I have done. It's like a car that isn't broken, but it isn't driving exactly right. If you want to keep it, you have to take it in to get fixed and be without it for a while. I am that car, and this is my maintenance time.

I love you with every fiber of my being, but I cannot continue to love you more than I love myself. You will be the love of my life until the day I die, and I pray you never doubt that. God bless you, heal your heart, and keep you safe always.

By September, I was miserable. I was continuing to battle with my anger and grief regarding the previous eighteen months. Gabe stopped talking to me and replying to my texts in that month. In addition to losing Daddy and Gabe, my career wasn't going so well. I continued crying out to God.

You have me more desperate than I've ever been in my entire life. I don't have my daddy to turn to anymore, and my husband left. I begged you to take me home last February because I knew I would never be the same after those three days. I know everyone says I'm here because you have a purpose for me, but I don't understand how this shell of a person can do anything for you now.

Going through those two tragedies separately is tough enough. [But I had to go] through them at the same time and then had them compounded with multiple medical issues, losing someone to suicide, and my miscarriage. I'm not Job, and I don't know how to move on. I feel stuck, lost, and empty. I feel like a burden to my real friends because I've been in this rut for *so long*. I know even in the midst of everything I am blessed and have it better than a lot of people. Yet I'm always on the verge of tears, and I truly feel as though I'm drowning.

Lord God, I know you have been carrying me since February 12, 2010. I will never forget the feeling I had all day that something was wrong. When Nicole found Daddy on the couch, my soul was crushed. I was already a mess because three days earlier Gabe said he wanted a divorce. I had already stopped eating, and then I just felt like my world ended that day. How am I supposed to keep going? You know, I thought I would run out of tears after all of the crying I've done. Yet they keep flowing.

Now, I get pulled back to the squadron that wants my head on a platter to deal with people's dirty looks and attitude. It's worse than high school. I used to love my job, and I was so proud of the career I chose. Today, I just want out, and I feel like it is all for naught. Where do I go from here?

God, I know I'm not what I've done but what I've overcome. I just need *your* strength to overcome and help others who may be able to be helped by what I've been through. You've got me desperate. I'm on hands and knees begging for *your* help. My life is in disarray, and I'm tired of hearing I'll be okay. I know you're my only hope. You've put me on a path I don't understand.

Be merciful, Oh Lord, for I am in distress; my eyes grow weak with sorrow, my soul and my body with grief. Because of all my enemies, I am the utter contempt of my neighbors; I am a dread to my friends—those who see me on the street flee from me. I am forgotten by them as though I were dead; I have become like broken pottery. But I trust in you, O Lord; I say, "You are my God." My times are in your hands; deliver me from my enemies and from those who pursue me. Let your face shine on your servant; save me in your unfailing love.

Psalm 31:9, 11-12, 14-16 (NIV)

Blessed is he whose transgressions are forgiven, whose sins are covered. Blessed is the one whose sin the Lord does not count against them and in whose spirit is no deceit.

Psalm 32:1-2 (NIV)

Help me, God, to break this hold and find myself. I'm struggling and trying to give it all to you. Take these burdens from me, Lord. I am casting all my cares on you!

One night that month I couldn't sleep. Thoughts ran through my mind like, *Why do I sabotage every relationship in my life?* None of my truly close friends could have said I never tried to ruin our friendship at some point, whether intentional or subconsciously. It's as if I thought because of all the bad things that have happened to me I didn't deserve any good. Or maybe I wanted to see who would truly stick around and love me after doing horrible things. I didn't really know or understand why I did this over and over again. Yet I continued to do it.

I continued to cry out to God in my suffering.

> God, why did you allow me to lose my husband and Daddy at the same time? I'd told/warned people for years that I didn't know how I'd survive when my daddy passed away. The multitude of nightmares about Daddy dying that started around age eight put a dread in my heart that never went away. That was my greatest fear for more than two decades. Then I met the love of my life.
>
> For the first time, I felt the same panic for someone else. Then I had to face both of them at once! Am I truly supposed to recover from those losses? *No one* will ever understand the relationship I had with my daddy. I still can't truly talk about him without crying. I can hardly see these sentences I'm typing because

of the tears pooling in my eyes and rolling down my face.

God, you gave me an earthly father that loved me the way you do. I had a perfect example in him of *you*. I feel so lost without him. I miss his voice, his gentle way, and his all-consuming hugs.

I don't know if anyone can understand what I've been through and how hard it is to completely give myself to another person. Saying I have trust issues is an understatement. I cannot put into words the damage that has been done to me from all of the abuse. I finally trusted someone and allowed him to know everything in my past. I wanted it to work more than ever before, and I gave my all, only for him to easily walk away after I sabotaged our marriage. I will own up to my mistakes and horrible screw-ups, but why wouldn't he fight for me? God, am I not worth fighting for?

Over those nineteen months I wanted to be like Sandra Bullock in *Hope Floats*. I wondered, *Couldn't I crawl into bed and not come out for months?* Unfortunately, I wasn't rich enough to walk away from my job and do that. I had ten days to mourn my marriage, Daddy passing away, and planning his funeral before returning to work.

I'm not a psychologist, but I'd say that wasn't enough time to even begin to deal with or grieve those two tragedies. In fact, I'm sure that was the reason I still felt stuck almost two years later.

I cried to God for hours many nights. The next morning I always had to wake up and pretend to be strong through my nine-hour workday. Then I'd return home and do it all over again.

It was not easy for a person who hardly ever cried before to become a walking waterfall. I wasn't a fan of crying uncontrollably over something little or the pain my heart felt every time I broke down.

Some days I wished I were rich enough to live on a tropical island alone until I chose otherwise. I'd cried and begged over and over for God to help me let go. I learned after all of the abuse I was a control freak. I didn't know how else to react. I felt cut off from everything. It seemed like no matter how sincere my heart was in asking God to take this burden from me, it was not good enough.

I was desperate for my heavenly Father to take control and help me. I truly had no idea what to do. I prayed, "Lord God, how do I cast all of my cares on you? I feel like I pray this constantly, and I'm getting nowhere! *Help me* not be miserable anymore. Fake it till you make it just isn't working."

I met with a chaplain for a counseling session. I knew I needed to make changes or I'd never get over Gabe. On September 8, I sent Gabe this letter:

Gabe, you know I love you, and I have been willing to do anything to prove it. I am not sure what happened for you to stop talking to me and to block me on Facebook out of the blue. It doesn't really matter because it all stops here! I will not be the cowering dog or whipping boy for you anymore. I am a strong woman, and although I know I did something wrong, I will not allow you to treat me like this. I have apologized and asked you, your parents, and God for forgiveness.

So here it is. As your wife, I never should have had to compete with your parents. Our marriage should have been you, me, and God (Genesis 2:24). The moment you went against your word and told your parents what happened, you handed our marriage to them, and I never stood a chance. You chose to trust them more than God. God brought us together. He changed my deployment, the country, and the timeline to take me to you. There is still no doubt in my mind he has a beautiful miracle planned for us, but you would have to trust him alone.

Therefore, I am not here for you to use for sex or companionship when you choose. You cannot have it both ways! You cannot appear to please your parents and still see me on the side. So until you trust God alone and choose to work on our issues with a chaplain and re-establish our relationship, these games are over. I would love to work through this and experience God's miracle for us. I would love to be your wife again and treat you like my king under God, but I will not be a weak person or allow you to treat me badly. You fell in love with me as a strong, godly, and fascinating woman. Why would you ever want me to be anything less than that?

As I said before, I will not be here for you to use. You must choose to trust God and talk to a chaplain with me or give everyone else what they want. God is faithful, and he is giving you the freedom of choice: God's way or the world's way (Malachi 2:16). So if you cannot go against your parents and you do not have any desire to have me in your life or to reconcile our relationship, we must say good-bye.

I love you and will never hurt you again. I will pray for you always.

Tiffany Dawn

The Love of My Life

My True Companion

My One and Only

Perfect for Me

"Red Strokes"

epilogue

After reading through my old journals, I can see I'm doing a whole lot better now. I still have difficult days and moments when I struggle even though it's two years after the death of my father and divorce from Gabe.

That season of my life was as dark as an Alaskan winter. I had no purpose, drive, or cares, as if I was stranded in the snow knowing my hours were numbered. I don't feel that way now. I'm still trying to figure out God's plan for my life, but at least I don't wake up every morning asking God why I'm still alive.

My wounds are still healing, but I'm slowly working through them. By the grace of God alone, I'm getting much better. There's no other way to explain it. It might've been easier if I had friends who lived close by. That way when I was having a hard day I could've said, "We should go grab dinner. I need to vent." I believe God orchestrated things that way so I'd learn to depend on him in an even greater way.

Not long after losing Daddy I had a revelation. I went to him for everything. I constantly leaned on my father for even the smallest things, such as questions about getting my car registered. If I didn't go to him, it was my husband.

Early on after my double dose of losses, I felt God gently say, "You will learn to depend on me." It kills me that he had to go to such an extent to get my attention. I needed to learn to lean on God primarily and others secondarily.

I'm grateful that I can see a difference between then and now. Before, nothing in me would've been sad to leave this earth. Now I have hope even though life isn't perfect. Part of the positive change came out of the process of writing about my journey. It enabled me to realize how far I've moved forward and how faithful God truly is!

In the Old Testament, God's older followers told each new generation what the Lord did in the past. This not only taught children God's ways but also reminded the adults too. Each time I share my story, I am able to not only help others see God's faithfulness but also be reminded of it myself.

Gabe never responded to the letter I sent him. I didn't even get a chance to tell him good-bye before he left for Korea in November. We have not exchanged any communication since August 2011. When I'm watching a movie at night, I sometimes forget that Gabe isn't there with me. I got used to my husband being present. Even though he hasn't sat by me for a while, I still miss him horribly.

God is still by my side, though, as I work through the pain of losing my husband. I made a clean break with him so that I could work on healing myself. Following through with letting him go is a daily battle.

> You will succeed in whatever you choose to do,
> and light will shine on the road ahead of you.
>
> Job 22:28 (NLT)

Although Mom was cancer free, she had lost so much weight, and pneumonia plagued her. Her fragile body, at approximately seventy-five pounds, lost the ability to fight. My mother told me shortly before she passed away that she gave her life to Jesus. She didn't want to die, but she had peace about where she would be. On the evening of January 19, 2012, my mom passed away. I am thankful she is no longer in pain and that we were able to speak on Christmas.

Many knew of our tumultuous relationship, but they are not aware of our final conversation. I made sure to let her know that I was happy she had found someone who made her happy and, even though we didn't speak often, that I did love her and was thankful she found the Lord.

She tried to apologize for things in the past. I told her it was in the past and I had forgiven her long ago. Regardless of the relationship we had, it was not easy losing my mom. We didn't get along as two individuals very well, but I did love her, and she will be missed.

My best friend, Nicole, and I decided to invest in a couple of new online businesses. We wanted to look at other opportunities for us to be successful and that would enable me to get home. I had to be able to pay my mortgage, or I couldn't just walk away from the air force.

From there, things began falling into place. A childhood friend named Andre was starting the two online companies. Andre called me about this great opportunity for Nicole and me.

I started praying for God to lead me in the right direction. I didn't want to get excited and run after anything. All three of us had been praying about the online companies and were determined to stay focused on God. Nicole and I sent Andre our checks. To make sure we were keeping God in the forefront, Andre tithed 10 percent before doing anything else.

Andre told me one day on the phone, "I've been trying to get this off the ground for a couple of years, and things just didn't work out with investors and stuff."

We agreed that God was in this and things were falling in line like we all needed. I began to feel more and more at peace regarding leaving the air force. I prayed from the get-go that we focused on God and that I would continue to tithe and trust his path. We turned our three business partners into four and expanded beyond what we initially considered possible.

I know God has perfect timing. I am trying to be patient, but I have never been known to be a long-suffering person. I am ready to go to Texas and get moving on my new path, but things are proceeding slowly with the air force.

Missy and me today

Currently, I am waiting to see the outcome of my evidentiary hearing, and I have come to learn they are looking for something else. I have never felt so betrayed by the job I once loved. In my mind, this has truly become a witch-hunt, and I just get to wait and see what transpires. Whatever may happen, God has a plan that will work for my good.

Over the last two years, I have lost the most important things in my life: my daddy, my husband, and now my career. God only knows why I am not a drug addict or alcoholic selling myself on the streets like the statistics say I should be after what I have been through. To me, there is only one reason I am alive and the person I am today. God. When no one else was around or could comfort me, and I was left and abandoned by the ones I loved most. He never left my side.

My story is ongoing, and I am still working on getting out of the air force to start on my new path. I know God has not brought me through all of this to leave me stranded here in the unknown.

I would not be alive today without God's love and compassion. In the last two years, I have seen the darkest times, and I never thought I would survive losing my dad and my husband. I never wanted to live past the day my husband left, and I begged God to take me home millions of times over the last two years. For some reason, I am still here, and I take that to mean he isn't done with me.

We have more things to do for my good and his glory. He carried me when I couldn't walk, and he has never given up on me no matter how many horrible things I have done.

People will let us down because we are human and none of us are perfect, but God will never leave us or forsake us. I am living proof of that. During some of my lowest times I took strength in these verses. I hope they bring you the same comfort they brought me.

> So be strong and courageous! Do not be afraid and do not panic before them. For the LORD your God will personally go ahead of you. He will neither fail you nor abandon you.
>
> Deuteronomy 31:6 (NLT)

The LORD himself goes before you and will be with you; he will never leave you nor forsake you. Do not be afraid; do not be discouraged.

Deuteronomy 31:8 (NIV)